W9-BBW-051

COUNTIES OF
CENTRAL
MARYLAND

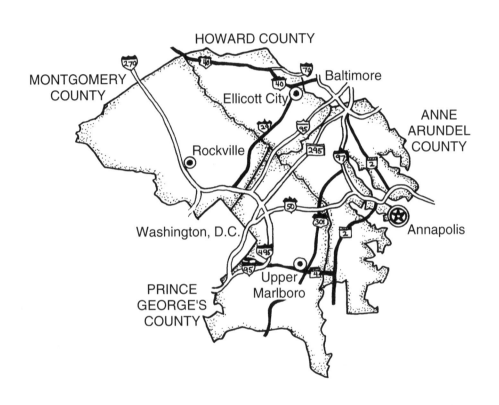

OUR MARYLAND COUNTIES SERIES

COUNTIES OF CENTRAL MARYLAND

by Elaine Bunting & Patricia D'Amario

Tidewater Publishers
Centreville, Maryland

Library of Congress Cataloging-in-Publication Data

Bunting, Elaine
    Counties of central Maryland / by Elaine Bunting & Patricia
D'Amario. — 1st ed.
      p.   cm. — (Our Maryland counties series)
    Includes bibliographical references and index.
    ISBN 0-87033-503-0
    1. Maryland—Juvenile literature.   2. Anne Arundel County (Md.)—
Juvenile literature.   3. Prince George's County (Md.)—Juvenile
literature.   4. Montgomery County (Md.)—Juvenile literature.   I. D'Amario,
Patricia. II. Title.   III. Series: Bunting, Elaine
Our Maryland counties series.
F181.3.B86   1998
975.2—dc21   98-26671
                                                                                    CIP

Manufactured in the United States of America
First edition

To all those students we have taught
and to all those who will read and learn from these pages

CONTENTS

PREFACE xi
CHAPTER 1. **Overview of Central Maryland** 3
   Geography and Climate 3
   Wildlife 6
   Plants 7
CHAPTER 2. **Early Central Maryland** 8
   Native Peoples 8
   Exploration 10
   Conditions in Europe 11
   Settlement by Europeans 12
   Trouble in the Colony 18
   Establishment of Towns 22
   Establishment of Roads and Transportation 23
CHAPTER 3. **Revolutionary Times** 29
   Land to the District 34
CHAPTER 4. **The War of 1812** 35
CHAPTER 5. **Slavery, the Civil War, and**
     Events That Followed 38
   Slavery 38
   The Underground Railroad 41
   The Civil War 42
   After the War 47
CHAPTER 6. **The Early Twentieth Century** 51
   Transportation 52
   World Wars I and II 53

Other Wars. 57
CHAPTER 7. **The Late Twentieth Century** 58
   Lifestyles 58
   Transportation 59
   Courts and Public Service Agencies. 60
CHAPTER 8. **Anne Arundel County (1650)** 66
   Establishment of the County 66
   County Seat 67
   Growth in the Twentieth Century 67
   County Government. 68
   Major Towns 69
   Churches and Religion 70
   Education and Schools 71
   Businesses, Industries, and Agriculture 74
   Fascinating Folks (Past and Present) 75
   Natural Resources 79
   Places of Interest 80
   Parks and Recreational Areas. 90
CHAPTER 9. **Prince George's County (1696)** 92
   Establishment of the County 92
   County Seat 93
   Growth in the Twentieth Century 95
   County Government. 95
   Major Towns 96
   Churches and Religion 97
   Education and Schools 98
   Businesses, Industries, and Agriculture 100
   Fascinating Folks (Past and Present) 101
   Natural Resources 104
   Places of Interest. 104
   Parks and Recreational Areas 107
CHAPTER 10. **Montgomery County (1776)**. 109
   Establishment of the County. 109
   County Seat 110

Growth in the Twentieth Century 110
County Government 111
Major Towns 111
Churches and Religion 112
Education and Schools 113
Businesses, Industries, and Agriculture 115
Fascinating Folks (Past and Present) 115
Natural Resources 118
Places of Interest 119
Parks and Recreational Areas 121
CHAPTER 11. **Howard County (1851)** 123
Establishment of the County 123
County Seat 124
Growth in the Twentieth Century 124
County Government 125
Major Towns 126
Churches and Religion 127
Education and Schools 128
Businesses, Industries, and Agriculture 130
Fascinating Folks (Past and Present) 131
Natural Resources 133
Places of Interest 133
Parks and Recreational Areas 136
BIBLIOGRAPHY 138
INDEX 140

Anne Arundel County Seal

Red and gold are the official county colors. The gold is taken from the coat of arms of the Calverts, the family name of the Lords Baltimore, and the red from the coat of arms of the Crosslands, George Calvert's mother's family. George Calvert was the first Lord Baltimore.

Prince George's County Seal

This seal, designed in 1696 by Charles Beckwith from Patuxent, represents Queen Anne and the countries of France, England, Scotland, and Ireland. The crown represents England's imperial crown. *Semper eadem* is Latin for "ever the same."

Montgomery County Seal

Designed by the College of Arms in London, England, this seal was adopted in 1976. The gold fleur-de-lis (an artistic design of a lily flower) and the gold rings with blue gemstones on the shield are from the Montgomery family's coat of arms. *Gardez bien* means "guard well."

Howard County Seal

Edward Stabler designed this seal in 1840. Tobacco and wheat, depicted in the center, were the two most important crops in the county at that time. The rolling hills of the county are shown in the background.

PREFACE

The first settlers came to the shores of what would become the state of Maryland in 1634. Eventually, there would be twenty-three counties in the state. This book is about the Central Maryland counties: Anne Arundel, Prince George's, Montgomery, and Howard. The four Central Maryland county seals are described to the left and illustrated in color on the back cover.

In preparing this book we visited the counties, interviewed people, and went to museums, historical societies, visitors' centers, historic buildings, chambers of commerce, courts, libraries, and the Maryland Hall of Records for information. We used books, newspaper articles, magazine articles, pictures, pamphlets, historical documents, the Internet, and personal interviews to research the book.

Fun Facts have been included to make the book more enjoyable and to give information that is surprising, funny, unusual, or particularly interesting in some way.

Our thanks to the staff of the Maryland Archives Hall of Records in Annapolis.

In Anne Arundel County: Thank you to the staff of the Anne Arundel County Public Library on West Street in Annapolis; June Ader and Lillian Kail, Annapolis Visitors' Center; Anne Peecook, receptionist, County Executive Office; Larry Telford, assistant to the county executive; Sue Portis, Anne Arundel County Sheriff's Department; Janice Dunleavy, District Court Administrative Office; June Mitchell, Office of Economic Development; Robert Wallace, court administrator, Circuit Court; Howard Hall, Retired Teachers' Association of Anne Arundel County; and Karen Cronin, Jug Bay Wetlands Sanctuary.

In Prince George's County: Thank you to Elaine Pickeral and Craig Moore of the Prince George's County Public Library in Upper Marlboro; Linda Hook, Prince George's County Court Administrator's Office; Barbara Holtz, Prince George's County Administration Building; Anne Holtz, Prince George's County Tricentennial Office; Fred DeMarr, Prince George's County Historical Society; Warren Rhoads, Prince George's County Historical Society; Anne Meredith Howes, Prince George's County Extension Service; and Teresa McCain, University of Maryland Public Relations Office.

In Montgomery County: Thank you to Susan Helmann, Natural and Historical Resources Division of the Maryland–National Capital Park and Planning Commission; Jane Sween, Montgomery County Historical Society; Tyler Peter, Circuit Court of Montgomery County; Melissa Warren, Montgomery County Chamber of Commerce; and Cindy Rupp and Judy Malamud of the Montgomery County Public Library in Rockville.

In Howard County: Thank you to the staff of the Howard County public libraries at Ellicott City and Columbia; Marada Cornwell, Circuit Court Clerk's Office, Civil Division; Kim Randall, Circuit Court Clerk's Office; Karen S. Justice, executive director, Howard County Tourism Council; Richard D'Ambrisi, volunteer (and historian) at the Ellicott City B & O Railroad Station Museum; Paul Bridge and Ed Williams, volunteers at the Ellicott City B & O Railroad Station Museum; Brandi Chavis, Columbia Association Welcome Center; Don McIntosh, Howard County author and historian; Doris Chickering, Lou LeConte, Anita Cushing, and Lyle Buck, Howard County Historical Society; Susan Lyons and Meg Gerety, Howard County Chamber of Commerce; Betsy Heger, Howard County Cooperative Extension Service; Fritz Lages, Columbia Soccer Club; and Dave Brinker and Marilyn Mause, Maryland Department of Natural Resources, Wildlife and Heritage Division.

Also thanks to Charlene Branch, WBAL-TV Channel 11, Baltimore; and Joyce Kashima, Public Affairs Department, WJZ-TV Channel 13, Baltimore.

And thank you to Evelyn Bunting and Helen Huebel for the information they found and the encouragement they gave us.

COUNTIES OF
CENTRAL
MARYLAND

CHAPTER 1

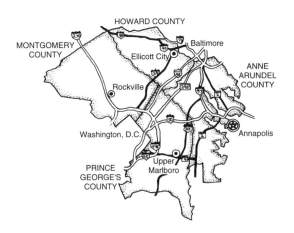

OVERVIEW OF CENTRAL MARYLAND

The Central Maryland counties of Anne Arundel, Prince George's, Montgomery, and Howard are located between the two important metropolitan areas of Baltimore and Washington, D.C. More people live in these four counties than in any other region of the state.

This central area is greatly influenced by how close it is to the Chesapeake Bay. The Bay and its many rivers and streams affect the food supply, occupations, travel, and recreation of the people who live there. The area's weather and climate are also affected by the Bay.

Geography and Climate

Anne Arundel County is on the Atlantic Coastal Plain and has fairly flat land, with sandy soil.

Montgomery, Howard, and parts of Prince George's County are three of the eight Maryland counties forming the Piedmont Plateau of

3

Maryland. This plateau is a large, hilly land area consisting of very old, hard rocks where streams have cut through deep, narrow gorges.

<table>
<tr><td>FUN FACT</td><td>Anne Arundel County is the only county in the United States with that name. However, there is a Montgomery County in Alabama, Arkansas, Georgia, Illinois, Indiana, Iowa, Kansas, Kentucky, Mississippi, Missouri, New York, North Carolina, Ohio, Pennsylvania, Tennessee, Texas, and Virginia. Howard is the name of counties in Arkansas, Indiana, Iowa, Missouri, Nebraska, and Texas. There is a Prince George (not Prince George's) County in Virginia.</td></tr>
</table>

Some of the best farmland in Maryland is found in the Piedmont region, where crops such as tomatoes, hay, wheat, corn, potatoes, and oats are grown.

Central Maryland has a moderate climate with distinct changes of seasons. The hottest days are usually in July and the coldest usually in January. Rainfall is generally sufficient for growing crops such as corn, soybeans, wheat, and tobacco. The average annual precipitation is 38.4 inches, allowing for a growing season of approximately 200 to 220 days without a killing frost in the eastern section. This is due to the warming influence of the Chesapeake Bay. There are 150 to 200 days of growing season in the western section.

<table>
<tr><td>FUN FACT</td><td>Hard rock, like granite and marble, is found in the Piedmont. Some hard rock from Ellicott City in Howard County was used in building the Naval Academy in Annapolis and the Washington Monument, the Capitol, and the Library of Congress building in Washington, D.C. Early colonists also used these rocks for building their homes.</td></tr>
</table>

Anne Arundel County is about 40 miles long and 20 miles wide. It has 418 square miles of land with mostly sandy soil. There are many creeks, streams, and rivers giving it 432 miles of shoreline and 7 square miles of water. The Severn, the Patapsco, the Magothy, the West, and the South Rivers run through the county.

Anne Arundel County is on the Atlantic Coastal Plain. It has elevations ranging from sea level at the Chesapeake Bay to 317.6 feet above sea level near Laurel. South of the South River, the county is more rural than in the north, where the urban sprawl of Baltimore and Washington has reached into the county.

Prince George's County measures about 20 miles wide and 30 miles long. It has 485 square miles of land and 11 square miles of water. Elevations range from 10 to 420 feet above sea level. Its highest areas are in the northern part of the county.

This county is on the peninsula of Southern Maryland. Its northern border follows the fall line, which divides the Atlantic Coastal Plain from the Piedmont Plateau. The fall line is marked by higher land elevations and many rocks and waterfalls in the rivers. Most of the rivers and streams are tidal (meaning that the water rises and falls with the tide) and move slowly through the large valleys. In the northern Piedmont Plateau part of the county, the streams flow more quickly. The county has rich soil, which is good for agriculture. Loam, gravel, sand, and iron are useful natural resources.

Montgomery County has a land area of 495 square miles. One third of its land is agricultural, and 27,321 acres of land are parkland. There are 10 square miles of water area in the county. The elevation ranges from 340 feet in Bethesda and Silver Spring to 512 feet at Gaithersburg.

Howard County, at 251 square miles and 160,640 acres, is Maryland's second smallest county. One small section of the county is on the Atlantic Coastal Plain. It has fairly level land and sandy soil. This coastal plain area runs along the southeastern part of the county roughly along U.S. Route 1. The rest of the county is part of the Piedmont Plateau. It has gradually rising elevation and fertile soil, which is good for agriculture. The elevation ranges from 50 to 850 feet above sea level, but most of the county is between 300 and 700 feet above sea level.

The yearly precipitation in Howard County is 43.4 inches. The yearly snowfall is 24 inches. The average summer temperature is 72.5 degrees, and the average winter temperature is 32.4 degrees.

Howard is the only county that is completely surrounded by other Maryland counties. It is sometimes called the heart of Maryland.   *FUN FACT*

Wildlife

There are many different kinds of wildlife in Anne Arundel, Prince George's, Montgomery, and Howard counties.

Many common varieties of birds are found in the Central Maryland region. These include robins, owls, sparrows, catbirds, crows, wrens, and blue jays. There are shorebirds such as ducks, gulls, terns, ospreys, egrets, herons, and geese. Rarer birds such as American eagles, swans, double-crested cormorants, cedar waxwing, sora rail, wild turkeys, ruby-throated hummingbirds, and Baltimore orioles are also found in this area.

Common mammals in the region are deer, bats, chipmunks, foxes, rats, mice, muskrats, opossums, woodchucks, beavers, raccoons, groundhogs, and squirrels. Some more unusual mammals found here are river otters, long-tail weasels, southern flying squirrels, minks, coyotes, and southern bog lemmings.

Reptiles and amphibians in the area include turtles (like stinkpot, box, red-belly, snapping, and painted), snakes (such as worm snake, black racer, ringneck, eastern hognose, king, garter, copperhead, and corn), and lizards (including racerunner, five-lined skink, and fence lizard). There are also salamanders (like marbled, spotted, two-lined, four-toed, red-backed, mud, and red), frogs (such as northern cricket, gray treefrog, spring peeper, upland chorus, bullfrog, green, pickerell, wood, and southern leopard), and toads (including American, Fowler's, and spadefoot).

Butterflies common to the Central Maryland region include monarchs, American painted lady, swallowtail, skipper, cloudy wing, and dusky wing.

There are thirty-nine known species representing seventeen families of fish in Central Maryland waters. Some of these are largemouth bass, minnow, pumpkinseed, American eel, hickory shad, mummichog, bay anchovy, brown bullhead, striped bass, tessellated darter, yellow perch, mosquito fish, hogchoker, and common carp.

Crabs, clams, and oysters are harvested and sold throughout Maryland and other states around the country. These shellfish are very important to the economy of Central Maryland.

Plants

Anne Arundel, Prince George's, Montgomery, and Howard counties have two types of forests. These are moist deciduous woods and dry, sandy, pine woods. Examples of trees found in moist deciduous (trees that drop their leaves in the fall) woods are chestnut, black walnut, quaking aspen, butternut hickory, tulip poplar, sycamore, oak, maple, cherry, ash, elm, alder, beech, and redbud. Evergreens include holly, pine, cedar, and spruce.

Some shrubs, bushes, and vines in the area are lilac, wild rose, bayberry, mulberry, gooseberry, blackberry, huckleberry, raspberry, grapevine, poison ivy, honeysuckle, staghorn sumac, clematis vine, and morning glory. The many wildflowers include wild licorice, goldenrod, black-eyed Susan (the state flower), foxglove, lady's slipper, dandelion, buttercup, vetch, Indian pipe, sunflower, and forget-me-not.

Clover, ferns, cattails, thistle, wild stawberries, and grasses are a few of the other plants growing in the Central Maryland region.

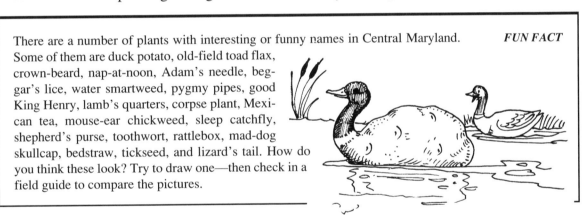

FUN FACT

There are a number of plants with interesting or funny names in Central Maryland. Some of them are duck potato, old-field toad flax, crown-beard, nap-at-noon, Adam's needle, beggar's lice, water smartweed, pygmy pipes, good King Henry, lamb's quarters, corpse plant, Mexican tea, mouse-ear chickweed, sleep catchfly, shepherd's purse, toothwort, rattlebox, mad-dog skullcap, bedstraw, tickseed, and lizard's tail. How do you think these look? Try to draw one—then check in a field guide to compare the pictures.

EARLY CENTRAL MARYLAND

Native Peoples

As long as thirteen thousand years ago, people lived in Central Maryland. The area's archaeological past is usually divided into four time periods: the Paleo-Indian (11,000 to 8000 B.C.), the Archaic (8000 to 1000 B.C.), the Woodland (1000 B.C. to A.D. 1600), and the Historic (A.D. 1600 to the present).

There are more recorded prehistoric archaeological sites found in Anne Arundel County than in any other county in Maryland. This is because prehistoric Indians made great use of the abundant resources such as deer, nuts, leaves, roots, crabs, and oysters. Archaeologists have found remains of these resources in soil at sites around the county.

FUN FACT	The woolly mammoth was among many now-extinct varieties of animals present in this area during the Paleo-Indian period.

During the Archaic period, the climate became warmer and drier. Melting polar ice caps flooded the Susquehanna River, which, in Maryland and Virginia, widened to create the Chesapeake Bay. The Indians invented new tools during this time—pointed weapons, axes, and stone bowls. The bow and arrow came into use during the Woodland period. Fishing for oysters became very important as a major food source.

The remains of a large group of Woodland period Indians have been found in what is now called the Beck Site in Anne Arundel County. This is an archaeological site that overlooks the tributary of the nearby Patuxent River. This site is considered so important that in 1983 the county purchased it to be sure it would be preserved.

During the Historic period, the land that would become Anne Arundel County was used as hunting grounds by various tribes of Indians. The Susquehannocks came down from Pennsylvania, and the Piscataways from Southern Maryland also hunted here. There were often disputes among the Indians as to who had rights to the land. Villages were built near rivers to make travel easier.

Captain John Smith drew maps of the Chesapeake region showing locations of many Indian villages along the Patuxent and Potomac Rivers; however, he never actually saw any of these villages. Some village names on his 1629 map include "Wasmacus," "Monanauk," "Nacotchtanek," and "Pawtuxant."

FUN FACT

Yocacomicos, Anacostians, Piscataways, Senecas, and Patuxents were tribes who lived in what would become Central Maryland. They considered it their sacred duty to be kind and hospitable to peaceful strangers. They were just the opposite toward their enemies, treating them with cruelty or killing them. They also punished members of their tribe if they were caught stealing, lying, or cheating.

The Piscataways built small huts and preferred to live as separate families. The Anacostians built long houses because they preferred to live together. The homes were made from tree bark or rush mats stretched over long wooden poles cut from trees. Both types of homes had holes in the roof above the fire to let out the smoke. These villages were usually protected by a stockade. The Piscataway men wore nothing on their heads and hung a blanket loosely over their shoulders. The women wore short skirts fastened tightly around their hips. This made it easy for them to walk through the woods or work in the fields.

The tribes of this area loved to dance. They formed a circle with a leader whom they followed. Men and women both danced, but never spoke to each other as they danced. Only the warriors danced the war dance. It was danced before or after a battle, or both.

The Indians got their food by hunting and fishing. Before the white man came, they hunted with bows and arrows. After the settlers came, they were able to get rifles to use when they hunted buffalo, bears, deer, and turkeys.

When an Indian died it was the job of the old women to bury him because the young people hated that job. He was buried with his weapons and other belongings. The women cried over the dead person. The loudness of their crying told how important he was, how much they had loved him, or how much he suffered when he was dying.

Exploration

It is thought that Spanish explorers sailed up the Chesapeake Bay during the 1500s. They left no records, so we have no information about them. However, one of the most famous English explorers of all time did come here and left very detailed records. Captain John Smith and his men explored the Bay and some of its rivers on two trips from Jamestown, Virginia, in 1608. They explored the Severn, the Potomac, and other rivers in the Central Maryland area. The captain's trips were not without hardship. His first trip ended earlier than he wished when his men took sick, and he was stung by a stingray in the Bay.

Conditions in Europe

At this time rulers in Europe began to establish colonies in the New World. Captain John Smith's journals, as well as those of other explorers, told of the exciting new continent. King James I and kings of other European countries, such as Spain, realized that sending people to colonize the New World would increase their wealth and power over rival countries. Kings began granting large tracts of land in the New World to wealthy friends. King James I of England granted lands to be colonized by people such as Sir Walter Raleigh and George Calvert. These men were expected to find investors (people to spend money to start the colony) and colonists (people to go to the New World and settle there).

Between 1550 and 1650 the population in England almost doubled. There were not enough jobs for everyone. With the population growing, many people had little hope of finding a job. Living conditions were terrible for these people. There was no indoor plumbing. People and their homes (if they had one) were very dirty. There was much disease, hunger, and death. Many people were desperate enough to travel to unknown lands, so the European colonists settled along the east coast of the New World, from what is now New England to Florida.

Settlement by Europeans

The area that is now Central Maryland was first settled in 1649 by three hundred Puritans lured away from Virginia by the promise of religious freedom. Maryland was the only colony that offered religious freedom backed by the Religious Toleration Act of 1649. This was passed by the Maryland General Assembly at St. Mary's City in St. Mary's County. It said all religions were to be accepted. The Puritans left Virginia because they did not have the freedom to worship as they wished. They were also trying to escape the high taxes in Virginia.

The Puritans were a religious group who used the Bible to guide their lives. They did not agree with the Church of England or the Catholic Church or any other religion that was not their own. They wanted to change other religions to meet their standards. This did not make them very popular with other people. During the 1600s, the Puritans began putting more and more pressure on the kings of England to reform the Church of England. As they gained strength, they were able to take over England and the Maryland colony for a while.

Puritan leaders Richard Bennett and William Durand contacted the governor of Maryland (who lived in St. Mary's City) for permission to settle here. The Puritans settled near the end of the year 1649. They claimed 250 acres of land on the Severn River on what is now Greenbury Point. They called their settlement Providence. The area where they settled included what eventually became Annapolis, the state capital.

The Puritans were probably very pleased with their new home. There was a mild climate. Hunting and fishing were good, and shellfish were also plentiful. There were no roads yet, but it was easy to get from place to place by boat on the many rivers and streams. The soil was good for growing tobacco, which was the major crop other than food.

Salaries were paid in tobacco, and goods and services were bought with tobacco. When a person had a large quantity of tobacco, it was packed into huge barrels called hogsheads and rolled to the wharves (docks). Each colonist had an agent in England to whom this tobacco was shipped. The agent exchanged the tobacco for coin money. He bought items needed by the colonist, such as clothing, shoes, furniture, and food supplies not available in the colonies. These items were then shipped back to America to the colonist.

Eventually more people came and settled in the area. Some of these were indentured servants. An indentured servant was a person whose passage to the colonies had been paid for by a "sponsor": someone already here or someone coming on the same boat as the indentured servant. The servant then had to repay the price of the trip by working for his or her sponsor for three or four years. After that time, the servant was free to go his or her own way, buy property, or start a business. Indentured servants were an important source of help, particularly on tobacco plantations. Three-fourths of the people who came to the New World started out as indentured servants.

Within one year, there were enough people in the settlement that the Maryland General Assembly decided to make it a county—Maryland's third. It was called Anne Arundel County.

Settlements in Anne Arundel County occurred quickly, with tobacco plantations established along most waterways. Not much is known of these plantations or the people who lived there, even though Maryland was England's largest, most populated colony at that time.

Most early homes had one, two, or three rooms. While not many have been excavated (dug up), it is known that many of them were "earthfast." This means they were built directly on or in the ground without foundations. This was a fast, cheap way to build. The colonists planned to replace them with better houses later when they could afford to, but many died before they could rebuild. Earthfast homes continued to be built in Anne Arundel County into the eighteenth century. In the 1720s, people began to build stronger houses of all sizes. Because they could not afford to build better houses, some people still built small homes with dirt floors and no chimneys.

FUN FACT	Remains of the buildings that existed in the seventeenth century are now buried, waiting to be discovered by archaeologists.

Settlers came to the area that is now Prince George's County in the 1600s. They chose their land and settled along rivers and streams. They built simple homes and cleared land to plant vegetables and tobacco. Life was very hard. There were no stores or roads. People traveled mostly by water in boats and dugout canoes. As time passed, roads were cut through the forests. More settlers came and the population of the area grew. The tobacco they grew, which they called sotweed, was sent to England in exchange for sugar, tea, clothing, furniture, and other goods. Many farms had docks where ships could land and collect the tobacco. These ships brought news, goods to buy, and sometimes mail, so the families looked forward to their arrival.

The earliest settlement in Montgomery County was in 1650, led by a man named Robert Brooke, who started a Protestant settlement with forty people, including his wife and ten children. They called their settlement Della Brooke. It was located on the Patuxent River.

The earliest Montgomery County settlers built homes of fieldstone with sod roofs. Sometimes they made shingles for their roofs from the cedar trees in the area. The chimneys were made of fieldstone. The settlers sometimes built springhouses in which to store butter, milk, and other foods that could spoil easily. Springhouses were cool inside because they were built over the very cold water bubbling up from the ground.

Later, when people had made and saved money, they began to build houses with bricks made from clay found in the area. Sometimes they used rocks that had been brought from England as ballast on ships.

(Ballast was used to make ships heavier and to stabilize them so they would not tip over.)

As with other settlements in the Maryland colony, common crops were tobacco, corn, and fruit, such as peaches and apples. Fish, oysters, and wild ducks came from the waters close by the town. People used tobacco to trade for what they wanted. In 1732, tobacco was worth one penny per pound.

The Quakers (or Society of Friends) were an important religious group of settlers in Montgomery County. In 1728, James Brooke was the first Quaker to build a house in the county. It was called Brooke Grove. Instead of services in a church, Quakers held what they called meetings at Brooke Grove. Their patience, intelligence, and strict beliefs about right and wrong and being fair made the Quakers a good influence on other settlers.

Because there were no street names at that time, settlers named their properties. Interesting land-grant names in Montgomery County were Girl's Portion, Clean Drinking, Bear Neck, Bear Bacon, Dung Hill, Thompson's Hop Yard, Gidding's Hah! Hah!! Two Brothers, Pork Plenty, If No Thieves, Errors Corrected, and Trouble Enough Indeed. Naming a property was necessary because it was the only address and was needed to receive mail.

Since there was no mail delivery system in the early 1700s, letters were sent by passing them from person to person. Each person, after receiving a letter for someone, would jump on a horse and speed it to the next settlement, and the next person would do the same, until the letter got to where it was supposed to go.

FUN FACT

When people started moving to what is now Howard County, they staked out farms for themselves where they could grow tobacco and food and have a few farm animals. These people did not want to live in towns, so towns were very slow to be established. In fact, it was not until after the Civil War (which ended in 1865) that communities began to grow. There were only two early towns of any importance: Elk Ridge Landing and Ellicott's Mills.

The earliest settlement in the area was Elk Ridge Landing, now known as Elkridge. It is located on the Patapsco River. It was a port where plantation owners and farmers brought their tobacco to be shipped overseas. Elk Ridge Landing was located just below the fall line, where the Atlantic Coastal Plain gives way to the Piedmont Plateau. Just beyond this point, the rocks and waterfalls on the Fall line prevent ships from going any farther up the river.

The establishment of iron furnaces and forges at Elk Ridge Landing caused the settlement to grow. This industry provided jobs to any settlers who did not want to farm. Later, in the 1800s, the railroad came to Elk Ridge. Farmers then had another, faster way to ship their crops to market, and travelers enjoyed the fast service. The railroad led to more growth in the area.

The first land grant in the area was 100 acres of land given to William Ebden in 1670. Ebden named his property Hockley. Another early grant was called Morning Choice, which became the home of a well-known iron industry family, the Dorseys. It is now known as Belmont.

Elk Ridge Landing was as important a harbor as Annapolis. (Remember, at this time, this area was still part of Anne Arundel County.) Then the Ellicott brothers came to the the county. Due to their influence, many farmers stopped growing tobacco and started growing wheat. The brothers built a town, as well as their mills, and Ellicott City was born.

The Ellicott Brothers

The Ellicott brothers came to the area in the early 1700s and started a mill. Andrew, Joseph, and John moved to the area from Pennsylvania in 1771–72, after searching other areas in Maryland for a good place to build a gristmill. At that time the area was still frontier. There were, however, farms nearby. The brothers convinced farmers in the Baltimore and Washington area to stop growing so much tobacco and switch to grains. They offered to transport the grain for them, and built a road to do so. They bought the grain from the farmers, ground it, and transported it to Baltimore, where they sold it. This was important to many of the farmers who had been growing tobacco for some time. Tobacco takes minerals out of the soil and leaves the soil infertile. Many of the farmers had been planning to leave the area and move to find more fertile land. Thanks to the Ellicott brothers they were able to stay and actually make a good profit growing wheat instead of tobacco.

Moving all their belongings from Pennsylvania to the Patapsco Valley was very difficult for the Ellicotts because there were few roads. They had to bring wagons, farm implements, horses, and building tools as well as their household goods. They also brought men to help them build the mill. The lower mills were built first. Then in 1774, Joseph Ellicott built the upper mills three miles away.

The first gristmill the Ellicott brothers built was very large: 100 feet long and 36 feet wide. It was the largest mill of its kind in colonial America. It had five pairs of millstones that were five feet across. How tall are you? If you are not yet five feet tall, these millstones were bigger than you.

FUN FACT

The Ellicotts also built other buildings, such as a log boardinghouse for workers and their families, a sawmill to cut lumber, a school, a courthouse, and a stable. They built a store that sold goods from as far away as New York and Philadelphia. There was also a post office in the store, and it was a gathering place for local people to come and get the news of the day. Other people began moving to the area and a town grew around the mills. Eventually, a Quaker meetinghouse was built. It was built on the highest point of land in the town, showing the importance people placed on their religion.

At one time there were as many as seven mills operating in the Ellicott City area. These mills produced animal feed, flour, iron nails, oil, lumber, paper, wagons, and wool. The mills were built on the river to use it as a source of power. However, the destructive floods along the river eventually closed the mills. A flood in 1868 killed fifty people and caused at least $1 million worth of damage. Many homes and businesses along the river were washed away.

In 1791, Joseph Ellicott's son, Andrew, a well-known surveyor, was asked to survey the boundaries for the new nation's capital of Washington, D.C. He did this along with Benjamin Banneker, the

Ellicotts' student and friend. Although Banneker is best remembered for the survey, he did not stay to complete the job. When Andrew Ellicott's two younger brothers joined them to work on the survey, Banneker returned home.

<table>
<tr><td>FUN FACT</td><td>Joseph Ellicott and his wife Judith took in six orphaned children of a friend who had died. They also had nine children of their own. That gave them fifteen children to raise. Can you imagine having fourteen brothers and sisters? When they grew up, four of the Ellicotts married Evans children, the orphans with whom they were raised.</td></tr>
</table>

The Ellicotts actually lived on the Baltimore County side of the Patapsco River, but without them, Howard County's Ellicott City would never have been built. They are considered to be a vital part of Howard County's history.

Early County Governments

In colonial times, counties were divided into governmental and religious areas called hundreds and parishes. Though the parishes were religious areas, their boundaries were established by the general assembly. These boundaries were different from those of the hundreds, which were political boundaries. The hundreds were established by the justices of the courts of each county and were used for taxing, voting, and other purposes. As population in the counties grew, new hundreds were established. The person in charge of the hundred was known as a constable. His job was to keep the peace, organize searches for wanted criminals, issue warrants for arrest, and keep tax lists.

Trouble in the Colony

The Puritans had come to Maryland for the religious freedom offered by Cecil Calvert, Lord Baltimore. In 1649, Maryland's General Assembly had passed an Act of Religious Toleration that offered religious freedom for all ". . . who professed a belief in Jesus Christ."

Even though the Puritans had come here to take advantage of the Toleration Act, once they were here they wanted to do away with it. Soon, they were opposing the colony's government. They wanted

everyone to worship their way, and they wanted to run the colony. They would not take an oath of allegiance to Lord Baltimore, because they believed that taking oaths was forbidden by the Bible.

There were violent clashes between the Puritans and the Catholics. On March 24 and 25, 1655, the Puritans and about one hundred of Lord Baltimore's men fought a bloody battle near what is now Annapolis. Lord Baltimore's men lost the battle and the Puritans took over the colony. They repealed (did away with) the Act of Religious Toleration and made their religion the only legal one. Catholics were not allowed to practice their religion openly. (The Lords Baltimore and many of the early settlers were Catholic.)

The founding of Maryland and its first seventy years occurred during much unrest and change in England. At this time, the Puritans had also taken over the English government. A man named Oliver Cromwell was in charge. Finally, after four years of trying, Cecil Calvert, a Catholic, was able to persuade Cromwell to give the Maryland colony back to him. In 1658, Maryland was again owned by the Calverts. Freedom of religion returned, and everyone could worship as he or she pleased. An agreement was made to return all confiscated lands to the Puritans. Pardons were granted to all who had participated in the war.

In 1661, Cecil Calvert, Lord Baltimore, appointed his son, Charles, to be governor of Maryland. One of Charles's accomplishments was to divide the Eastern Shore into counties. By 1674, Maryland had ten counties. They were Somerset, Kent, Talbot, Cecil, and Dorchester on the Eastern Shore, and St. Mary's, Anne Arundel, Charles, Baltimore, and Calvert on the western shore of the Bay.

A Royal Colony

In 1675, Cecil Calvert died. Charles Calvert became the third Lord Baltimore. He was still serving as governor when the colony was again taken away from the Calverts, this time by the Protestants, who had taken over England. The new king and queen of England appointed Sir Lionel Copley to be Maryland's first royal governor. Religious freedom again vanished.

The Moving of the Capital

In 1694, Francis Nicholson became royal governor. He made one of the most important decisions in Maryland history. He decided to move the capital of Maryland from St. Mary's City to Anne Arundel Town. This town had grown up near the early Puritan settlement. St. Mary's City was not central to the colony and was hard to reach. Soon, the name Anne Arundel Town was changed to Annapolis, which means "city of Anne." It was named for Princess Anne of England, who eventually became queen. Annapolis has been Maryland's capital ever since.

Work and Play in the Colony

Early colonists did not shop at supermarkets or department stores. They also had no movies, television, or computer games for entertainment. They had to make, grow, or hunt everything they ate, used, or wore. There were many things to do, but the colonists divided the work among members of their households. Children often worked as hard as their parents. They were taught from an early age how to do the many tasks that needed to be done on the homestead.

Men and boys went hunting and fishing. They built furniture for the house and took care of livestock and the major crops on the farm. They built canoes and wagons and cut firewood for heating and cooking.

Women and girls cared for the kitchen garden, in which they grew vegetables and herbs for the family. They prepared flax (wool) and spun it into thread. The thread was then woven into cloth and made into clothes, curtains, or quilts. They made soap, candles, and butter. They did all the cooking and washing of clothes.

People worked from before sunup until after sundown. They did find time to enjoy themselves, frequently combining work and play with their neighbors. These neighbors would help them with difficult or time-consuming tasks. Husking bees were parties held in the barn to husk and shell corn. Women held quilting bees to make quilts by hand. They also had feather stripping parties where they would strip the down from feathers to fill pillows and feather beds. There were house and barn raisings. The colonist would prepare the logs and put the frame of the house or barn together. Then a large group of people would get together and help him "raise the house." The women and girls would prepare food for everyone helping at the raising.

Cards were popular in some areas of the colonies. It was against the law to sell cards. Adults sometimes played card games, but children were never allowed to play.

Children enjoyed themselves playing marbles, tag, checkers, fox and geese, blindman's bluff, and hopscotch. Fishing, swimming, and ice skating also were popular.

The children liked singing games and rounds such as "London Bridge," "Here We Go 'round the Mulberry Bush," "Ring around the Rosie," and "I Put My Right Foot In." When their mother could take a few minutes away from her housework, she helped them make popcorn and taffy. Colonial children had few toys; most were handmade. Popguns were made from the wood of elder trees, bows and arrows from hemlock, and whistles from chestnut or willow trees. The children also made their own dolls, tops, and hoops.

 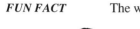

Establishment of Towns

The first town in Anne Arundel County was Providence, the settlement of the Puritans from Virginia. Annapolis soon developed near there, and it is the only city in Maryland whose charter was issued under the royal seal of England. Governor Seymour granted the charter in 1708, in the name of Queen Anne. Land along the north shore of the Severn River was settled in the seventeenth century. At first the land in Anne Arundel, Prince George's, Montgomery, and Howard counties was used mainly for farming tobacco and other crops. Then small settlements of people who did not wish to farm began to appear. Some, like Linthicum in Anne Arundel County, grew up around plantations. People who settled in these towns were shopkeepers, tavern owners, blacksmiths, wheelwrights, and millers. There were eventually general stores, churches, harness shops, and inns. Taverns were popular meeting places. Sometimes towns would grow up around a particular business, such as a mill. Rockville, in Montgomery County, grew up around a tavern.

Many of Montgomery County's suburbs were originally sold as resort locations. Therefore, many hotels were built in the areas of Bethesda, Forest Glen, and old Chevy Chase.

Bethesda Park was an amusement park that opened in 1891. It was once advertised as "the handsomest park in America" and "the biggest success ever known." The park had a small zoo, plant garden, dance hall, roller coaster, and Ferris wheel.

Before the Civil War, there were very small villages in Howard County. People had settled mainly on farms when they moved to the county, so towns were slow to grow. The villages of Elk Ridge, Ellicott's Mills, Ilchester, Marriottsville, Clarksville, Savage, Hilton, Elysville, Popular Springs, Mathew's Store, Cooksville, Owingsville, and Lisbon were all in existence. The villages grew up along the rivers or roads.

After the Civil War, some town names were changed. Ellicott's Mills became Ellicott City in 1867. Elysville became Alberton, and Mathew's Store became Glenwood. There were new towns as well, such as Woodstock, West Friendship, and Jonestown. These towns were still small, most having populations of fewer than 150 people. Ellicott City had the largest population, with 2,900 people in 1878.

Ellicott City received a grave blow in 1868, when a terrible flash flood washed away much of the town and killed fifty people. A huge wave of water swept down from the Mount Airy area on July 24, 1868. People had no warning and did not try to leave their homes until it was too late. Fourteen houses were swept away along with the Granite Factory, the Avalon Nail Factory, and other businesses. Every mill along the river was damaged, and many mills and other buildings were completely washed away.

NOT-SO-FUN FACT

Establishment of Roads and Transportation

The earliest transportation in the colonies was by water. Indians friendly with the colonists taught them how to hollow out logs to make dugout canoes. The trees were stripped of their branches, then hollowed out by burning and scraping. These Chesapeake log canoes were important in traveling and food gathering. Sometimes larger ones were made by using two or three logs. By 1880, there were more than six thousand of them in use up and down the Bay.

The first roads in the Central Maryland counties were Susquehannock and Piscataway Indian trails that followed the ridges of the hills. They were narrow and sometimes so muddy that they were impassable. Travelers also had to worry about robbers and hostile Indians.

Annapolis became an important port for ships. It had been a tradition for more than thirty years to entertain travelers there. During the 1600s, visitors who arrived by ship, stagecoach, or ferry enthusiastically referred to Annapolis as the most genteel city in the colonies. In addition, it was famous for its taverns. Two particularly well-known taverns were the Harp and Crown and the King of France. Many shops lined the streets, such as those of perukemakers (wigmakers), cabinetmakers, sailmakers, silversmiths, and tobacconists.

FUN FACT   Before 1750, it was impossible to take a carriage from Annapolis to Philadelphia because there were neither connecting roads nor bridges over the Bay and rivers.

Bridges were being built in the counties before the Civil War. Bridges over the Severn River, Spa Creek, and College Creek in Anne Arundel County were all built before the war.

The earliest roads in Montgomery County were dirt roads. They wound through forests and along streams. One of the earliest ran from Georgetown, near Washington, to Frederick. The first turnpike ran from Georgetown to Rockville. It was built by the Washington Turnpike Company and was completed in 1828.

FUN FACT   The first turnpike charged a toll for its use. Four cents was charged for a horse and rider, and twenty-five cents for a small herd of cattle or a carriage or wagon with two horses.

A stagecoach ran between Georgetown and Frederick every seven days. By 1800, it ran twice a week. It cost six cents per mile to ride the stage. One road in Montgomery County is built above a brick-lined tunnel that carried the water supply to Washington from Great Falls. The road used to be known as Conduit Road. It is now known as MacArthur Boulevard, named after World War II General Douglas MacArthur.

Early roads in Howard County, before and after it became a county, were unpaved. They were often winding and muddy. Some of the early roads were toll roads, such as the road from Ellicott's Mills to

Baltimore, which was called the Frederick Turnpike. Building of the road was begun by the Ellicott brothers. The amount of the toll paid depended on the number of people passing, the size of their coach or wagon, and the number of horses being used to pull it.

The Ellicott brothers also built and paid for a road to Charles Carroll of Carrollton's Doughoregan Manor, so that farmers could bring grains to Ellicott's Mills. This road was extended westward in the 1790s to Fredericktown. Landowners along the way helped to pay for this extension. This road later became part of the National Road, also called Cumberland Road. It is now Route 40.

Chesapeake Bay steamships served as cargo ships and passenger steamers. The passenger steamers were beautiful, large ships that could carry hundreds of people. Smaller steamers carried freight such as farm products. There were steamship landings on the Patapsco River, the Rhode River, the West River, and the South River in Anne Arundel County. Some creeks also had landings.

Travel by water was very popular because travel by roads was still very bad. Annapolis became a port of entry in 1668. This meant the merchant and cargo ships from overseas docked there, and taxes on imported goods were collected at the custom house. Annapolis continued to grow as a place to ship tobacco and other goods overseas. London Town, located on the South River, was also was a port of entry beginning in 1683. Travelers used it as a stopping point because it was halfway between Williamsburg, Virginia, and Philadelphia, Pennsylvania. These two ports welcomed ships bringing in goods from Europe and other places. They remained vital to Maryland until the 1790s, when Baltimore began to grow in importance as a port. Baltimore had deeper water than Annapolis or London Town, and larger ships were being built that needed the deeper water. Currently, archaeologists are digging in the remains of London Town. They expect to find as many as one hundred foundations from buildings that used to be there.

Steamboats first came to Prince George's County's Potomac and Patuxent Rivers around 1810. They became a very popular means of transportation. Tobacco was transported by steamboat from the county into Baltimore until the early 1900s. Goods were brought back from Baltimore to Prince George's County. There were several steamboat lines, such as the Weems Steamboat Line started by George Weems in 1817. One of the landings for this line on the Patuxent River served Upper Marlboro. It was called Hill's Landing.

Railroads

By the 1820s and 1830s, people were looking for a faster, safer way to travel than by horse or stagecoach. Therefore this time was one of great change for Howard County and all of Central Maryland. This was due in great part to the coming of the railroad. In 1828, the first section of line was started from Baltimore to Ellicott's Mills. Baltimore wanted to open a way for travel westward. It was hoped this rail line would compete with the C & O Canal, which ran along the Potomac River from Georgetown near Washington. The line, the first for the Baltimore and Ohio (B & O) Railroad, was 13 miles long. It began service on May 24, 1830. It was the first railroad line built in the United States.

FUN FACT The first trains were carriages or stagecoaches put onto rails and pulled by horses. Since the horses could not pull the train cars the whole 13 miles, a relay station was built midway with a stable for the horses. The horses were changed at this point. This is now the town of Relay in Baltimore County.

The first railroad station in America was built at Ellicott's Mills on this B & O line. It opened in 1831 and was used to load and unload freight. Later it also became the station for the first regularly scheduled passenger service in America. It is built of granite quarried in Maryland. The building is now a national historic landmark and museum.

In 1833, Andrew Jackson became the first American president to travel by rail when he boarded the train at Ellicott's Mills. Early trains might seem like toy trains today because they were so small. In 1863, a section of track was built at the terminal that could be moved around in a circle. This was to turn the trains around and point them back toward Baltimore. It was called a turntable.

Plans for this line were organized in Baltimore. Charles Carroll and other men on the board of directors decided to have the line follow the river and go to a mill town. A mill town would have grain, flour, and other goods to ship back to Baltimore. They chose Ellicott's Mills and that line opened in 1830. In 1835, a branch line was opened from Relay to Washington. This line required the building of the Thomas Viaduct, a 700-foot-long stone bridge with eight arches. It was designed by Benjamin Henry Latrobe, Jr., and could carry one hundred times the amount of weight it was built to hold. It was named after Philip E. Thomas, the first president of the Baltimore and Ohio Railroad.

In 1844, the first telegraph message in America was sent from Washington to Baltimore. The telegraph wire ran across the Thomas Viaduct.

People began building houses along the rail lines. They could get transportation, goods and services, and news. By 1852, the line ran all the way to the Ohio River, opening the door to the west.

FUN FACT

While railroad cars were still being pulled by horses, the steam engine was soon to follow. Its designers were confident that the steam engine could out-pull a horse. The story goes that in 1830, there was a race between one of these small steam engines and a horse-drawn railcar on the new railroad line between Baltimore and Ellicott's Mills. It is said that a belt on the steam engine broke near the end of the race and the horse won. Historians have not been able to find any real evidence that this story is true. However, there is some basis in fact for this story since this type of race probably did occur many times. Its importance is that it emphasizes the change from natural transportation (horses) to artificial power. Now people were in control rather than being dependent on horses for their transportation.

The small steam engine was given its name by a man named John H. B. Latrobe in 1868. He was giving a speech and mentioned "that Tom Thumb of an engine," naming it after the Tom Thumb of P. T. Barnum fame. Tom Thumb was a real person. He was a very small man whose actual name was Charles Sherwood Stratton (1838–1883). He joined P. T. Barnum's museum in 1842 and was known as General Tom Thumb.

With road travel so bad, Anne Arundel countians looked forward to a railroad. The first railroad line in the county was the Annapolis and Elkridge Railroad. Its first run was from Annapolis Junction to

Annapolis in 1840, using a steam engine. At Annapolis Junction, travelers could switch to the Baltimore and Ohio Line to continue their trip to Baltimore. The Short Line was another railroad line that opened in the 1880s. It allowed travelers to go directly from Annapolis into Baltimore without changing trains—a much shorter and faster trip.

In 1835, Prince George's County got one of the first railroad lines in the country. A line from the Baltimore and Ohio Railroad was built that year. It ran from Baltimore to Laurel to Bladensburg to Washington. At the point where this rail line met the Baltimore-Washington Turnpike, the town of Beltsville developed. In later years, other towns were established along the railroad.

On May 24, 1844, Samuel F. B. Morse sent a message from the Riversdale Estate in Prince George's County to Washington, D.C. Morse had been experimenting with the telegraph for twelve years, and this was the first message sent by the new method of communication. Some of his research was funded by the federal government, but the government did not run the telegraph system that developed. The telegraph was a success because it was simple to use and inexpensive. By 1851, there were many private telegraph companies.

Western Union Telegraph was one of the first telegraph companies to become successful. This company signed contracts with railroads to lay lines along tracks. Railroads also allowed telegraph offices in train stations. The railroads and Western Union worked well together. The telegraph made the railroads safer by coordinating schedules and helping relay word when there was trouble along the tracks.

The telegraph and the railroad were very important to both the North and the South during the Civil War. By the beginning of the Civil War, there were two main telegraph companies in the United States: Western Union and American Telegraph. Western Union's telegraph lines ran east and west and American Telegraph's ran north and south. By the end of the Civil War, only Western Union remained successful because many of American Telegraph's lines had been destroyed during the war.

| *FUN FACT* | Western Union became America's first industrial monopoly (the only company of its kind), and it was the country's largest corporation at that time. |

REVOLUTIONARY TIMES

Throughout the mid-1700s, people became very angry with England for taxing them but not allowing them to have representatives in the English Parliament (like our Congress) to speak on their behalf. Many people started thinking about becoming free from England and having their own government in the colonies. Not only people in Maryland began to think this way, but people in all thirteen colonies. The British were taxing goods coming into the colonies and closing ports if the taxes were not paid. The colonists called these taxes the Intolerable Acts. When they closed the port of Boston, Massachusetts, many people thought this was the last straw. On December 16, 1773, a group of men disguised themselves as Indians, boarded three ships in Boston Harbor, and dumped 340 chests of tea into the water. This was to become known as the Boston Tea Party. A similar incident took place in Anne Arundel County two months before the Boston Tea Party.

A man named Charles Carroll was probably the most important man in the county at that time. He was, without a doubt, the wealthiest man in Maryland. In fact, he was the wealthiest man in the American colonies. This, of course, made him very powerful and influential in Annapolis. He was involved in the following incident, probably saving some lives.

On October 19, 1774, the cargo ship *Peggy Stewart* was loaded with 2,320 pounds of tea, on which there was a tax. The citizens of Annapolis decided they would not pay the tax and would not let the ship dock. The owner of the ship, Anthony Stewart, and its captain tried to dock the ship anyway and paid the tax on the tea. A crowd of angry citizens gathered near the dock. Charles Carroll tried to avoid trouble by telling Stewart he should burn his ship to save his life and the lives of others who might be hurt in angry rioting. Stewart made the difficult decision that Carroll was right. He set fire to his ship, which was towed out into the Bay to burn. It sank off the area which is now the site of the U.S. Naval Academy.

FUN FACT The ship was named after Anthony Stewart's daughter, Peggy. She and her mother watched the ship burn from an upstairs window of their house. If you visit the Naval Academy, you can see a bronze plaque indicating the spot where the ship went down.

Opinion was greatly divided among Maryland colonists whether to remain under English rule or to fight for independence. Many people living in central Maryland had rejected the Church of England. So they supported fighting for independence from England. Representatives attended the Maryland Convention. On July 2, 1776, they passed an important resolution on independence from England. Realizing that war would happen soon, the convention appointed a troop of soldiers to serve for six months. These men were divided into four battalions, each with nine companies. Five of these companies came from Anne Arundel County, three came from Prince George's County, and two from Queen Anne's County. George Washington was named commander-in-chief of the entire Continental Army.

Four men from Maryland signed the Declaration of Independence on July 4, 1776, in Philadelphia. They were Charles Carroll of Carrollton (1737–1832, born in Annapolis, lived in Frederick County); Thomas Stone (1743–1787, born in Charles County); William Paca (1740–1799, born in an area of Baltimore County that became Harford County); and Samuel Chase (1741–1811, born in Somerset County). Only Charles Carroll was born in Anne Arundel County, but all four men built or bought homes in Annapolis.

There were no battles fought in Anne Arundel, Prince George's, Montgomery, or Howard counties, but there were some nervous days when the British warships were plundering towns along the Chesapeake Bay and its rivers.

At the time of the American Revolution, children were at great risk of dying, though not from the war. The death rate in the central Maryland area for children under five years old was 50 percent. They died of malaria, smallpox, typhus, measles, and cholera. If they lived to grow up, their life expectancy was only thirty-two years. Today, many people live into their eighties.

NOT-SO-FUN FACT

Prince George's County's greatest service in the war effort during the American Revolution was in providing guns and other supplies to American soldiers. Stephen West turned his plantation into a gun factory. Guns were also brought there to be repaired. In addition, West provided blankets, powder, woolen cloth, and other supplies needed.

A Prince George's countian important in the movement for independence was John Rogers. He was a member of the Continental Congress. On July 4, 1776, when the vote for or against the Declaration of Independence was taken, he voted for independence.

Rogers lost the congressional election that was held a few days later. Therefore, he did not sign the Declaration of Independence. The signing was held on August 2, 1776. Since that time he has been known as "the lost signer," since he is the only man who voted for the declaration who did not sign it.

NOT-SO-FUN FACT

Not everyone in Prince George's County was for independence from England. Reverend John Boucher used his pulpit at St. Barnabas Church to preach the evils of making war with England. His congregation became so angry that Reverend Boucher feared for his life. He started bringing pistols to church to defend himself. He finally decided it would be best to go home to England where he would be safe.

A person of great help to the colonists during the war was Thomas Attwood Digges. Digges lived in England during the war and served as a spy, secretly sending information to the Continental Congress. After the war, he moved back to Maryland to his family's estate, Warburton Manor, near Fort Washington.

FUN FACT   Thomas Digges was America's first novelist. His book was called *Adventures of Alonso*.

When news of the closing of Boston Harbor reached the citizens of Lower Frederick (now Montgomery County), they responded by calling a meeting in the old Hungerford Tavern. At that meeting they drew up a set of five resolutions (decisions everyone agrees on) called the Frederick County, Maryland Resolutions, also known as the Hungerford Resolves. The first resolution said they sympathized with the citizens of Boston. The second said that the blockade of Boston's harbor by the British was wrong. The third said no one should trade with Britain and the West Indies until Boston Harbor was open and Britain stopped taxing them. The fourth resolution appointed ten men to a committee to represent the county citizens at the General Committee in Annapolis. The fifth resolution was to send a copy of these decisions to Annapolis to be printed in a newspaper, the *Maryland Gazette*. These resolutions show that the colonists were very upset with Britain, but not yet ready to declare war. They were hoping the resolutions would change the mind of the king, and that he would stop the taxation and allow the colonists to have representatives in Britain. But the resolutions did not work.

In 1776, Hungerford's Tavern was designated as the county's courthouse because of its central location. After Montgomery County was officially established, the tavern was renamed the Montgomery County Courthouse.

Powder mills were built in Montgomery County to provide gunpowder and foundries to build cannons for the war. (At a foundry, metals are melted and poured into molds for building things, like a cannon.) One foundry, built by a Mr. Hughes on the Potomac River a mile from Georgetown, is where the first cannon in the country was made.

The American Revolution ended with the signing of the Treaty of Paris in September 1783. It was signed in Paris, France, by John Adams, Benjamin Franklin, John Jay, and David Hartley. The treaty was then delivered to the newly elected members of Congress in Annapolis for ratification (approval). At 12:00 noon on December 23, 1783, in the Senate Chamber of the Maryland State House, George Washington resigned his commission as commander-in-chief of the Continental Army. The treaty ending the war was ratified on January 14, 1784. Annapolis then served for nine months as the capital of the new United States.

George Washington often visited a tavern in Annapolis called the Tuesday Club. The specialty served there was known as "fish house punch."

FUN FACT

Big changes took place after the American Revolution, which had more of an impact on Anne Arundel County than the war did. Many of the loyalists (people still loyal to England) packed up and went home to England. They felt strange living in a country not governed by Britain. Many of these people had been wealthy and had held positions of leadership in the county. Their leaving opened these posts to others. Farmers bought more land as the large plantations were divided up and sold.

After the Revolution, there was much debate about what kind of government our new country should have. A Constitutional Convention was held in Philadelphia to write a constitution that would give us a strong, democratic government. The Constitution was finally signed on September 17, 1787. One of its signers was Daniel Carroll of Prince George's County. Once it was signed, it was given to the states for ratification. Maryland ratified this new constitution on April 28, 1788. It was the seventh state to do so.

Land to the District

In 1791, it was decided to have a district where the capital of the United States would be located. This would be a separate area from the states, and would not be considered a state. Land was given by Maryland and by Virginia for this district. The Maryland land given came from Montgomery and Prince George's counties, with the most coming from Prince George's northwestern corner.

FUN FACT	While the District of Columbia was to become self-governing, for the first nine years it remained under the leadership of Prince George's County.

In 1800, the governing of the District was taken over by Congress, and Prince George's County was left with the area it covers to this day.

THE WAR OF 1812

Following the American Revolution, most Americans believed they could live peacefully with all nations. Coastal defenses were abandoned and navies disbanded. At the same time, due to harsh working conditions on British ships, hundreds of British sailors were deserting their navy. Many found work on American ships, so the British Navy began boarding American ships to remove these sailors. They also took some American-born sailors, which angered the Americans. In 1807, when the British frigate *Leopard* fired on the American frigate *Chesapeake* near Norfolk, Virginia, Congress voted for money to fortify thirty-three seaports, including Annapolis. The defense system at Annapolis was to include two forts, Fort Severn and Fort Madison. Fort Severn later became the site of the Naval Academy, established in 1845.

An enemy could not maintain an army on land without a harbor at which to land men and supplies. When war with England did come, the Annapolis garrisons were increased, and local militia began preparing to fight. British ships were often sighted in Chesapeake Bay waters. It

35

was believed they planned a major attack on Annapolis and other areas. Twice in 1813, the Anne Arundel militia was called out to prepare for threatened invasions. It wasn't until June 1814 that a British fleet positioned itself off Annapolis to prevent American privateers (armed private ships) from escaping. They stayed for two months, then sailed away to join the rest of the British fleet waiting in the Patuxent River. After burning the capital, Washington, the British fleet traveled up the Chesapeake Bay headed for Baltimore. As they approached Annapolis, many citizens thought they planned to invade their town. People abandoned their homes and headed for the countryside with their belongings piled high on their wagons. They soon realized the British planned to attack Baltimore, rather than Annapolis. Major William Barney counted the ships from atop the State House dome and sent messengers to warn Baltimore of the impending attack. The British again passed Annapolis as they left the Bay after their defeat at Baltimore. The end of the war came three months later with the signing of the Treaty of Ghent.

FUN FACT	Many artifacts from the War of 1812 can be found at the Naval Academy in Annapolis. One of these is the flag from the downed frigate *Chesapeake*, on which a dying James Lawrence inscribed "Don't give up the ship." This later became the navy's famous watchword.

One of the battles fought during the War of 1812 is one that Marylanders would like to forget. The Battle of Bladensburg, in Prince George's County, on August 24, 1814, was fought between the British and a very unprepared group of Americans. The American soldiers were trying to save the city of Washington from being attacked. The British sailed up the Potomac and Patuxent rivers. At Bladensburg they met the troops, who had very little training and no field commander.

Events associated with this battle led to the writing of the "Star-Spangled Banner." After fighting the Battle of Bladensburg and winning, the British marched to Washington, D.C. They burned parts of Washington, including the White House and the Capitol. On their way back through Prince George's County, the British attacked Upper Marlboro. British soldiers entered the home of Dr. William Beanes and dragged him out of bed in the middle of the night. They took his house as their headquarters and put him on a British ship. The ship was soon involved in the attack on Fort McHenry at Baltimore. Francis Scott Key went to Baltimore to try to rescue his friend, Dr. Beanes, which he was able to do. While on the British ship watching the bombardment of Fort McHenry, Key wrote the poem that became our national anthem.

Knowing there was no field commander, President Madison, the secretary of war, and even Francis Scott Key went to the battlefield to advise the troops, but they could not help. The Americans were defeated and the British marched on to Washington.

NOT-SO-FUN FACT

When the British burned the White House, the Capitol, and other parts of Washington, D.C., President James Madison escaped to the town of Brookeville in Montgomery County, thereby making this town the U.S. capital for a day. The town of Brookeville was established in 1794 and is one of the county's earliest settlements.

During the war, British ships sailed up the Chesapeake Bay and sent raiding parties ashore to steal from and annoy the citizens of counties along the Bay and rivers. The Fourth Brigade from the lower part of Montgomery County and the Seventh Brigade from the upper part of the county were called up to serve during the war. General William H. Winder commanded the troops from the county. His troops had few supplies, little food, and no tents.

CHAPTER 5

SLAVERY, THE CIVIL WAR, AND
EVENTS THAT FOLLOWED

Slavery

By the middle of the 1660s, the number of indentured and other servants coming to the New World could not keep up with the number needed. Many people decided not to leave Europe because they thought there was not enough land left in the New World. (Remember, most of the New World had not yet been explored by Europeans. In the 1600s, people had no idea that 3,000 miles of land continued west of the Atlantic Ocean.) Some indentured servants did continue to come. Most welcome were those with a skill, such as bricklayers, blacksmiths, and carpenters. Eventually, slaves were taught these skills. They took over these jobs where needed on plantations, because slaves were cheaper to buy than indentured servants.

Slavery became a fact of life in Central Maryland before the Civil War. Slaves were a source of cheap labor, which was so needed on the tobacco plantations of colonial Maryland.

The need for slaves became greater as indentured servants finished their terms and bought farms of their own. To successfully grow tobacco, plantation owners had to have a lot of cheap labor. When slave traders started bringing people from Africa and the West Indies, plantation owners decided this was the answer to their problem. Slaves were taken from their homes in West Africa to slave ports. They were held at the slave ports until ships came to take them to the New World. Once here, the Africans were sold at slave markets, including Upper Marlboro and Nottingham in Prince George's County and Annapolis in Anne Arundel County.

The slaves did a variety of jobs. Most slaves were farm workers, some worked in the tobacco fields. Others were trained as blacksmiths, carpenters, stable boys, house servants, ladies' maids, or nannies. Businessmen bought slaves to help with day-to-day work in their taverns, shops, and inns.

Slaves were frequently sold to other plantations, so it was very hard for them to have a home and family. Most slaves were able to see family members at other plantations. They could marry, though there was no guarantee that husband and wife would live out their lives together. Parents were often separated from their children. They were not allowed to learn to read and write. The slaves' owners believed that with education the slaves would be better able to plan escapes.

A slave's first name was often an English name given to them by their masters. Slaves were seldom given a last name. When they were freed they would sometimes choose the last name of their former master, or take the name of their skill, like Miller or Cooper. Sometimes, they took the name of a well-known person they admired. Some of the names taken by slaves in Howard County were Dorsey, Addison, Snowden, Cooke, and Brown.

Often, slaves tried to escape, heading north toward Canada where they would be free. After the American Revolution, the spirit of freedom inspired some white people to write articles and poems in the newspaper encouraging slave owners to free their slaves. The Quakers in Maryland refused to own slaves. They were an important religious group that encouraged others to free slaves. Many slaves were freed during this time, but many were not. They were still important to the economic security of the counties. Of the ones who were freed, most stayed in the area to be near relatives who were still slaves. Some were able to start small businesses, buy small farms, or make money from jobs. When they had enough money, they could buy relatives out of slavery.

In 1789, the Maryland Assembly seriously considered a bill that would have laid out a plan for freeing slaves in Maryland over a period of time. The bill was introduced by Charles Carroll of Carrollton. Unfortunately, Carroll was appointed to the federal Senate, which met in New York. He could not be in Annapolis to encourage passage of his bill. The bill "died in committee," which means nothing was done about it, and slavery lasted another three generations.

The 1860 census (just before the Civil War) records 7,332 blacks still being held as slaves in Anne Arundel County out of a total population of 23,900 people.

In Prince George's County as in other places, without a large work force such as slaves, it was impossible to grow tobacco. Therefore slaves were used there also. Eventually some slaves were released by their masters in Prince George's County. By the 1860 census, of a total population of 22,272 people living in the county, 11,424 were black slaves, and 1,198 were free blacks. These people began to establish their own churches and schools and start their own communities. The former slaves worked as gardeners, house servants, carpenters, and midwives, and at other skilled jobs.

Many black communities in Montgomery County developed on land given to them by the Quakers and Methodists. Freed slaves began settling such land in 1826. In the eighteenth and nineteenth centuries, owning land and farming it was considered the best way to show a person was successful. So the Quakers and Methodists encouraged free blacks to improve their standing in the community by farming. Many blacks moved to areas where their Quaker and Methodist friends lived.

The Underground Railroad

The Underground Railroad was not a real railroad, with tracks and train cars. It was actually a secret group of people up and down the East Coast who believed that slavery was wrong. They helped slaves escape to the north where they could live in freedom. The stations on the Underground Railroad were the homes and barns of the "conductors," who directed the slaves to the next station on the Underground Railroad where they would find the next conductor.

Many slaves ran away simply to find other members of their family. One tragedy of slavery was that often families were separated when one or more members were sold.

Montgomery County had an extensive, secret Underground Railroad system. Slaves followed streams, such as Rock Creek, or small roads through the county as they traveled north. One road ran from Sandy Springs to Laurel. They hid in swamps and forests in the county. Some members of the Society of Friends (or Quakers) and some members of the Methodist faith became conductors to help the slaves. A large population of free blacks in the area of Georgetown, which was once part of Montgomery County, also helped in this effort.

One of the most successful conductors in Montgomery County was Jacob Bigelow. He worked for the Washington Gas and Light Company as a lawyer and secretary. In secret, he was one of the main conductors on the railroad. He used two routes that went through Rockville to help many slaves escape.

In 1857, a sandstone bridge was built across Cabin John Creek in Montgomery County. At that time, it was considered to be the largest single-span stone arch in the world. Legend says that the arch had a secret passageway in it where slaves were hidden, making it a part of the Underground Railroad.

Some people in the area that would become Howard County owned slaves. However, most Quakers, like the Ellicotts, strongly opposed slavery. In the 1790s, there were about 1,000 slaves in Howard County. By 1860, just before the Civil War, this number had more than doubled to 2,862 slaves. There were also a large number of free blacks living in the area. A major route on the Underground Railroad in Howard County was along U.S. Route 1 that led into Baltimore.

The Civil War

The Civil War was fought for a number of reasons, slavery being only one. The most important reason was to decide whether the Southern states should leave the Union and form their own separate country. When other states started leaving the Union, and war was drawing near, people in Maryland began taking sides. Because Maryland was a slave-owning state, most people thought the state would favor the Confederate (Southern) side. But Maryland's governor in 1861, Thomas Hicks (from Dorchester County), and other people in the government thought the states should remain together as one country. They were Union (Northern) supporters. So Maryland officially supported the Union cause.

When President Abraham Lincoln started organizing an army for the Union, some young men joined. But many Anne Arundel County men went south to Richmond, Virginia, or Charleston, South Carolina, to join the Confederate Army.

Since most white people in Anne Arundel County supported the Southern cause, federal troops were sent to Annapolis to keep order. In fact, martial law was declared across all of the western shore of Maryland because of the number of Southern supporters. Under martial law, military troops are in charge, and everyone must do as they say. The Union troops that occupied Anne Arundel County were under the leadership of General Benjamin Franklin Butler. He and his troops set up camp at the Naval Academy, and General Butler chose the City Tavern as his headquarters. General Butler was not a popular general, even among Union supporters. He was known as a violent man who thought he was always right, and everyone else was wrong. Everywhere he went, he was hated. When Governor Hicks heard that Butler was assigned to Annapolis, he wrote him a letter asking him not to come. Of course, he came anyway.

General Butler's job was to help troops coming from the north to get to Washington to protect the capital. Troops had been going through Baltimore, but there were violent skirmishes with Southern supporters there. One of the worst was on April 19, 1861.

A college teacher in Louisiana read in the newspaper about that clash between Northern and Southern troops in Baltimore. He was from Anne Arundel County, and one of the men killed had been a close friend of his. Grief stricken, he sat down and wrote a poem. On April 26, 1861, his poem, "My Maryland," was published for the first time in a Louisiana newspaper. After seeing it reprinted in a Baltimore newspaper, two sisters, Jennie and Hettie Cary, found that the words fit the music to the Christmas song "Tannenbaum, O Tannenbaum." The teacher and author was James Ryder Randall, and the song is "Maryland, My Maryland." The Cary sisters sang the song for Confederate troops in July 1861, at the Fairfax Courthouse in Virginia. After that, it spread throughout the state of Maryland. Today it is our official state song.

When you see the song written today, usually only the first three verses are printed. The rest of the song is considered too sad. Incidentally, most people who have been singing the song all their lives do not realize that the "despot" (cruel leader) in the first line of the song is President Abraham Lincoln.

To bypass Baltimore, Union troops were put on boats on the Susquehanna River in Cecil County and Harford County and sailed south to Annapolis. There they would march or ride the train to Washington. The people of Anne Arundel County tried to make troop movement harder for the Union Army by tearing up railroad tracks between Annapolis and Washington. They also took parts from an engine so that it could not operate. Some of General Butler's men were able to fix the engine and the track to get the railroad running again.

In November 1861, a new governor was elected. He was Augustus Bradford from Harford County. He was also a Union supporter, so his election did not change Maryland's stand in the war. Governor Bradford was governor for the rest of the war.

During the war, the counties were controlled by the Union army. The people resented it, but they carried on as best they could. Some were arrested, sometimes without cause, and without regard for their rights as citizens. For five years, the Central Maryland counties lived under military control.

The Union army had several prison camps in Anne Arundel County. One was Camp Parole, and another was at St. John's College. Another prison camp on Mt. Helena Island, off of what is now Severna Park, was called Mt. Misery by the prisoners.

On April 27, 1864, Governor Bradford held a Constitutional Convention in Annapolis. Confederate supporters opposed it, but the governor thought the state constitution needed rewriting to meet the changing times. Delegates went from all the counties. Delegates from Anne Arundel County were Oliver Miller, Sprigg Harwood, Eli J. Henkle, and A. S. Bond. The constitution written at the convention was not one that was popular with the people. Anyone fighting for the South was disenfranchised, meaning that he had no rights or privileges, such as holding office or voting. It also provided freedom for slaves with no payment to their masters. Although it was very unpopular, even with some Union supporters, this constitution is important because when it was passed on November 1, 1864, all slaves in Maryland were free as of January 1, 1865.

FUN FACT   The constitution that freed Maryland slaves came more than a year before the nation officially did away with slavery in the Thirteenth Amendment to the U.S. Constitution, on December 18, 1865.

Most people in Prince George's County were Southerners at heart. They had plantations, grew tobacco, and owned slaves, as people in other Southern states did. Abraham Lincoln was not a popular choice for president in the county because he favored doing away with slavery.

As war drew near, thousands of men joined the Confederate Army. Southern states, such as Virginia and North Carolina, declared that they were no longer part of the United States. President Lincoln stationed Union troops throughout Maryland to make sure the state did not join the Confederacy (made up of Alabama, Arkansas, Florida, Georgia, Louisiana, Mississippi, North Carolina, South Carolina, Tennessee, Texas, and Virginia). But most Prince George's countians did not want Maryland to leave the Union anyway. President Lincoln had promised Maryland slaveholders they could keep their slaves if the state remained with the Union. President Lincoln issued the Emancipation Proclamation in September 1862, by which blacks held in slavery in the Confederate states were declared to be free. This proclamation became law on January 1, 1863.

In April 1862, Washington, D.C., abolished (did away with) slavery in the District. Many slaves fled to Washington and freedom. Since many had also left to join the Union Army, the number of slaves in Prince George's County decreased drastically.

There were many soldiers in Central Maryland during the war. They guarded the rail lines and all roads into Washington, D.C. They built a number of forts. Fort Lincoln and Fort Foote were in Prince George's County. The troops noticed that early in the war most people in the county would not take sides and preferred to be left alone. However, later in the war, their support definitely turned to the South.

Captain Wat Bowie from Prince George's County was an officer serving the Confederate cause. The Union Army wanted to capture him so badly that they offered a reward for him. He finally was captured, but escaped. He was eventually killed in Montgomery County during a skirmish (small fight) with local Union supporters. In Rockville, a bronze statue of a young Confederate private stands as a monument to Confederate heroes.

There were no Civil War battles fought in Prince George's County. However, a large group of Confederate troops entered the county in July 1864. They blew up the railroad tracks at Beltsville and cut telegraph wires. They set up camp at the Maryland Agricultural College, now the site of the University of Maryland. The following day, they left the camp and joined in a battle in Washington, D.C.

During the Civil War, soldiers from both sides were frequently seen in Montgomery County. There were several skirmishes between Union and Confederate soldiers, including some at the town of Beallsville. Soldiers from the South were there to defend the county, and Union soldiers invaded on their way to Washington to defend the capital. Local people hid their food supplies and hid their favorite horses in cellars.

By the time of the Civil War, most of the Quakers had left the Howard County area. Some of the people still living there supported the North and some supported the South. In Ellicott City, most people supported the Union. Some farmers hid their horses in the woods so that Union troops could not steal them. Soldiers also sometimes stole food to supplement their diet of salt pork and hardtack. (Hardtack was a very hard biscuit or bread made from flour and water, with no salt.) Farmers who supported the Confederate troops sent money and supplies to help them.

Union forces considered the Thomas Viaduct, which carried the railroad line and the telegraph line, to be the most important target for Southern forces in Central Maryland. Fearful that it would be blown up or taken over by the Confederates, Union troops guarded it day and night. During the war, this was the only railroad route west from Washington. It was called the Old Main Line.

In 1861, the Union soldiers found out that Southern sympathizers were taking a large powerful gun from Baltimore to Harper's Ferry, Virginia. They planned to travel through Ellicott's Mills. General Butler of the North ordered his men to capture the gun. When the gun was taken, they could not get it to work. This was because the inventor, a Mr. Dickinson, had escaped in a buggy carrying all the important parts of the gun.

Finally, in 1865, the war ended and the Northern troops left. It was time to rebuild lives and look to the future.

After the War

Despite the battles fought between North and South, the union of America remained intact. A period of rebuilding followed, called Reconstruction. Many new things were invented between the Civil War and World War I that improved people's lives. Some of these were indoor plumbing, automobiles, electricity, radios, and central heating.

Before this time, people got their water from a stream or an outdoor pump or well, and they used fireplaces for heat.

NOT-SO-FUN FACT

Life was shorter at that time. People were killed by horses, fire, falling under the wheels of wagons or carriages, and wounds from tools and guns. By the end of the 1800s and in the early 1900s, people were expected to live only into their middle or late forties.

During this period, there were laws passed that segregated (separated) blacks and whites. They were segregated in schools, restaurants, neighborhoods, public bathrooms, and where they worked and played.

In 1867, Marylanders adopted a new constitution to replace the unpopular one written during the war.

Anne Arundel County continued to grow through the 1800s and early 1900s. The railroad was the main reason for growth in the upper part of the county. People could live in the county and work in Baltimore, Washington, or Annapolis. Many businesses moved into the area.

Not long after the Civil War ended, the tragic assassination of President Lincoln took place on April 14, 1865. John Wilkes Booth planned the deed in Prince George's County. A family named Surratt owned an inn in Surrattsville (now called Clinton), where Confederate sympathizers met and plotted against the Union Army. A few men had also met there to plan the assassination of the president, the vice president, the secretary of state, and General Ulysses S. Grant. However, President Lincoln was the only one to die as a result of the plot. Booth stopped at the Surratt House for a short time after the assassination when he was trying to escape capture. The men who had plotted with Booth were arrested and hanged in July 1865, as was Mary Surratt, the owner of the inn. John Wilkes Booth escaped and fled to Virginia, where he was cornered and shot by federal agents.

NOT-SO-FUN FACT

Many historians do not believe that Mary Surratt had anything to do with the plot to kill the president and others. Her daughter pleaded with the authorities not to convict her mother, but Mary Surratt was found guilty. She was the first woman to be hanged by the U.S. government.

The Civil War left Prince George's County's farms and plantations without slaves to plant tobacco and other crops. With no workers, the farmers and plantation owners could not grow enough crops to keep their farms going. The county became very poor. Large farms were divided into sections, which were then sold. A number of small farms remained, but many people moved into towns.

After the war, most of Prince George's County's former slaves became farmers. Families that had been torn apart when members were sold to other plantations were joyfully reunited. One such family was the Plummer family, who were slaves on the Riversdale Plantation near what is now College Park. The oldest daughter was sold to a plantation in New Orleans, Louisiana. The mother was sold twice to other plantation owners. Finally, after the war, the family was reunited and bought a small farm. They named it Rose Hill. One of the daughters, Nellie Arnold Plummer, wrote a book about the history of her family.

Other black families left the area right after the war. Many of them eventually returned and, by 1880, there were almost as many black families in the county as there had been just before the war. They started building communities with churches and schools. By the 1880s, there were a few people moving into the county who had jobs in Washington. They built homes near the railroad so that they could ride to work on the train. They were Prince George's County's first commuters. (Commuters are people who live some distance from where they work. Usually we think of someone who lives in the suburbs and who works in a city as a commuter.)

Among the people who moved into the county in the late 1800s were a group of people from Germany. Although there were not many of them, they were important to the county because they started new towns and businesses. They were the first Europeans to move to Prince George's County as a group since the British settlers who came when Maryland was still a colony.

FUN FACT

After the Civil War, Montgomery County was left in ruins. Troops that invaded from the North had used school desks and church pews for firewood. Soldiers from the North and the South had stolen livestock and horses and left the people sad and fearful. Families had been broken up by death and had very little money left.

By the 1870s, the economy began to improve with the arrival of the Baltimore and Ohio Railroad in the county. On May 23, 1873, the first steam train on the metropolitan part of the B & O Railroad crossed Montgomery County. Now goods, services, and passengers brought new industry along the railroad tracks. Tobacco and wheat were replaced by dairy farms, because the train could carry the milk quickly to market. New towns began to appear along the railroad, and trolley lines were built. This created a link with other towns. With the coming of steam power, sawmills began to operate.

After the war, gold was discovered in Sandy Spring, Rockville, Bethesda, and Great Falls. The largest amounts were found at Great Falls. Gold mining companies formed, all of which had closed by 1950.

In Howard County, the United Daughters of the Confederacy planned a monument to the fallen Civil War soldiers. Lack of money prevented them from having the monument built. It wasn't until after World War II that the monument was finally completed and dedicated. It is located on the grounds of the Howard County Courthouse in Ellicott City.

THE EARLY TWENTIETH CENTURY

In 1935, the federal government bought 12,000 acres of land in what is now the Greenbelt area. The land was to be used to build a "green town," one of several planned communities that were part of President Roosevelt's New Deal program. Besides the new town of Greenbelt, the land was also used for the Patuxent Wildlife Refuge and the Goddard Space Flight Center.

With the development of more and more industry from the 1940s through the 1960s, agriculture began to decline in the Central Maryland area. Factories and businesses replaced many acres of farmland.

In the mid-1960s, schools were desegregated to provide equal education for black children and other minorities. Before this time, black children and white children attended separate, but not equal, schools.

Transportation

In the early 1900s, many roads were still dirt covered. When it rained, the new "horseless carriages" (cars) often became stuck in the mud, and horses or oxen had to pull them out.

FUN FACT   The early cars did not have headlights because batteries had not been invented. To see better at night, drivers hung kerosene lamps near the roof of the car. Streetlights in towns before the 1920s were gaslights. A man called a lamplighter walked around lighting each one when it got dark. At dawn, he went back and snuffed each one out.

At this time, an electric train system came to Anne Arundel County. Railroad workers strung wire above the tracks to carry electricity to power the trains. The Washington, Baltimore, and Annapolis Electric Railroad Company served Anne Arundel County until 1950, when bus service took over. Today, Amtrak and MARC (Maryland rail commuter) trains help people in the Central Maryland counties travel quickly and conveniently. CSX and Conrail trains carry freight for businesses. Baltimore/Washington International Airport serves the state internationally. The counties also have bus service and light rail service. The light rail is a system of high-speed commuter trains that carry people from suburban areas into Baltimore and Washington.

Between 1910 and 1930, roads were built and paved. Before this, roads were either unpaved or paved with oyster shells. Many bridges were built across rivers to make travel quicker and easier. A section of U.S. Route 50 stretching from Washington, D.C., to the Severn River Bridge in Anne Arundel County was named after John Hanson. He was an important Maryland patriot during and after the American Revolution.

The first dual-lane highway in Maryland was the Governor Ritchie Highway from Annapolis to Baltimore. It was built in 1934 and paid for by the federal government. It was named for Albert C. Ritchie, who was governor of Maryland from 1920 to 1935.

World Wars I and II

During World War I, all men between the ages of eighteen and forty-five were expected to serve in the military. The Central Maryland counties struggled through the two world wars much like the rest of Maryland. There was gas rationing and food shortages. Businesses failed because people did not spend as much money as they normally did.

In May 1917, with the start of World War I, Congress authorized the establishment of Camp George G. Meade. It was a reception and training center for more than one hundred thousand recruits during World War I. Today it is known as Fort Meade.

The Fort Meade site was originally the location of Bethel Methodist Episcopal Church South, founded in 1890 by the Reverend John Nichols. The church and its original cemetery are still located on Fort Meade. There are nineteen cemeteries at Fort Meade. Some people even think that there is an Indian burial site at the Post Cemetery, which is the fort's military burial ground.

HERE LIES REV. JOHN NICHOLS

Fort Meade is located in the Odenton-Jessup area of northern Anne Arundel County. It is a 13,000-acre installation. Construction began on July 2, 1917. Builders put up 1,460 temporary wooden buildings that could house 42,000 men. They were replaced with permanent brick buildings between World Wars I and II, and the name was changed from Camp Meade to Fort George G. Meade.

NOT-SO-FUN FACT	The building of Camp Meade forced families from their homes and land. The federal government bought 19,000 acres of land to be used for training troops. Many people had owned their land since before the Civil War and hated to leave.

Before the camp was constructed, the area was rural. Although farmland was lost by establishment of the fort, it did help to develop the social and economic stability of the area. More people moved to the area seeking the jobs created by the fort.

Today, the National Security Agency is on the grounds of Fort Meade. This is one of the nation's most important government agencies. The people who work there gather information about the activities of governments and terrorist groups all over the world. The work that goes on there is very secret.

James Harris Rogers, an electrical scientist, was important to America's role in World War I. He lived in Hyattsville in Prince George's County. His main work was in the field of underground and undersea communications. He invented a system that allowed U.S. ships and submarines to communicate with each other. He also created a system that made it possible for Americans to listen to messages sent by the Germans. For his work, Rogers was nominated for the Nobel Prize. Rogers also served for six years as the chief electrician of the U.S. Capitol building.

Montgomery County held a going-away event for the men who were reporting to Camp Meade in Anne Arundel County. The men were given a dinner, speeches were made, and the soldiers were led by the King's Valley Band as they marched to the train depot to leave for war. The women at home also helped the war effort. Women were not allowed to fight, so many joined the American Red Cross, which was started by Clara Barton. They knitted socks for the men fighting in Europe. They made bandages and collected items the troops needed and sent them overseas.

In 1917, when the United States entered World War I, a group of Howard County women organized a Women's Preparedness and

Survey Committee and took part in a war bazaar held in Baltimore. They sold baked goods and canned preserves to raise money for the relief effort in Europe. Another group of women in the county organized themselves and learned to shoot guns. They wanted to be able to defend their homes if the need arose. They were organized by Augusta Kossman and were called the Minute Women of Harwood.

During World War I, children in Montgomery County held pageants to show their patriotism. They dressed up as Native Americans, Uncle Sam, Charles Lindbergh, and people from other countries. This was to represent some of the cultures in America.

Many teachers served during this war. Schools had difficulty finding enough teachers.

FUN FACT

The Patapsco Female Institute building in Ellicott City was turned into a hospital to care for returning wounded men. It was temporarily renamed the Maryland Convalescent Hospital for Soldiers and Sailors.

After peace was declared, a parade was held in Upper Marlboro to welcome the soldiers home. A memorial to people from Montgomery County who had died in the war was dedicated that day on the courthouse lawn. The town of Bladensburg erected Peace Cross to honor the war dead.

Just after World War I, a terrible flu epidemic hit Montgomery County. Many people got sick and even doctors were at risk. After three doctors in his area died, Dr. Jacob W. Bird opened a hospital because there was only one other in the area and it was privately owned. Bird's hospital got crowded so quickly that he bought another 12 acres of land and built another hospital, which he named the Montgomery County General Hospital. It opened in 1921 and is still serving patients today.

At the beginning of World War II, thousands of troops moved into Fort Meade. The National Security Agency was very active in gathering information on enemy activities and plans. More buildings were built. Many new businesses opened near the base.

During World War II, people raised money for the war effort. Some people paid to attend dances, and some people bought defense bonds. They grew their own food in gardens known as victory gardens. The

Red Cross was active in collecting money. Air-raid drills were held, for it was feared that the Germans might bomb the Washington area.

Between World Wars I and II, the first drive-in movie theater in Maryland was built in Anne Arundel County. The Governor Ritchie Open Air Theater opened in May 1913. It closed in 1980. The site is now a housing development.

As with most cities and towns in Maryland, air-raid wardens were appointed to serve in every neighborhood. Air-raid drills were signaled by a siren. During air-raid drills, each warden would check his neighborhood to make sure every window was blacked out (covered so that no light could be seen from outside). No one was allowed to carry a lighted match, pipe, cigarette, or cigar. If enemy planes flew over they would be unable to see anything. Because Montgomery County was so close to Washington, D.C., people were afraid the county could be hit with bombs if the capital was attacked. The government provided them with free sand to put out any fires that might result from these bombs.

Several places in Anne Arundel County were thought to be targets for the enemy. The National Security Agency at Fort Meade, the fort itself, and the naval radio complex on Greenbury Point were strategic places. People volunteered to patrol the beaches to watch for German planes, ships, or submarines. Families who had summer homes in the county rented them to military families. Luckily, these bombings never happened.

People stored water sealed in gallon jugs and kept canned foods and blankets in their root cellars. The root cellars became known as bomb shelters. The Red Cross stockpiled first-aid supplies, pumps, blankets, stretchers, and fire-fighting equipment. They also made bandages.

Thousands of men from the Central Maryland area served in World Wars I and II, and several hundred died.

After World War II, Howard County grew and grew. The suburbs spread out farther, with many people living in the county and working in Baltimore or Washington.

Other Wars

People from the Central Maryland counties have served in other conflicts since World War II. These include the Korean War, the Vietnam War, and the Persian Gulf War.

THE LATE TWENTIETH CENTURY

Lifestyles

In the late twentieth century there were many changes that greatly impacted people's lifestyles in the Central Maryland area as well as across the United States. Advanced technology, like the computer, was one of them. In the beginning, a computer filled an entire room and only the most knowledgeable people could operate it. Now, computers are used in cars, homes, offices, and stores. Housing also changed as some families moved from individual homes to condominiums. What had been called row homes became known as "townhouses." Other families left the crowded cities to live in the suburbs. Building booms occurred in the Central Maryland region as farmland was developed to accommodate the increasing population. The city of Columbia is an example of a large portion of farmland lost to development.

By the 1960s developers began constructing malls in these areas to provide shopping for people who had moved to the suburbs. These malls and other businesses provided many jobs to the new county residents. A shopping trip that used to require traveling to many different stores in the city could now be accomplished in one trip to a mall.

Because of the great number of theaters, museums, restaurants, national monuments, festivals, and other cultural events in Baltimore and Washington, D.C., wealthier people tended to move to this Central Maryland region to take advantage of them. People from around the world live here, many of whom work at the foreign embassies in Washington or for international companies like GTE and IBM.

Transportation

Ask any real estate agent (a person who helps others buy and sell property) and you will be told the three most important things about property are "location, location, and location." Anne Arundel, Prince George's, Montgomery, and Howard counties' locations are just about perfect for a variety of reasons. Most important is that they are located close to Baltimore and Washington. The transportation network in and between these cities is extremely important to these counties. Many businesses have located there. They need ways to move their products to markets inside and outside the counties. Also, many people who live in this region work in Baltimore or Washington.

As more and more people move to more distant suburbs, they have longer commutes to work. This creates a need for bigger and better highways. As a result, this area has an excellent network of roads and mass transit, including the Metro bus service and Metro rail system. Beltways and other highways have been constructed around the cities to make traveling easier. Route 495 is called the Washington Beltway, but it actually runs through Prince George's and Montgomery counties. This beltway was constructed for suburban travelers to drive from place to place without traveling through the city. Interstate 95, which connects with the Washington Beltway, runs through Howard and Prince George's counties. Developments began to spring up around these beltways, which then created more congestion (crowded highways).

There are several other large highways that run through Central Maryland and connect to the Washington Beltway. One is the

Baltimore-Washington Parkway, which runs through Anne Arundel and Prince George's counties. Another is Interstate 270 through Montgomery County. Routes 50 and 301 run through Anne Arundel and Prince George's counties. Interstate 70 runs from Baltimore City through Howard County to Western Maryland.

In Howard County, the greatest amount of development has occurred with the building of Columbia. Most of the roads there were built after the invention of cars. This has made driving around Howard County fairly easy, because the roads are wider and straighter than the old roads built for horses and wagons. The largest highways in Howard County are Interstate 95 and Interstate 70. Route 40 runs from Baltimore through Howard County, where it joins Interstate 70. Route 29 runs north and south from Route 70 to Washington, D.C.

Buses that serve Howard County pick up passengers at park-and-ride lots. In Columbia, the ColumBUS shuttles people between the city's villages. There are more than 50 miles of public pathways that wind through the woods, valleys, and open areas of Columbia.

Courts and Public Service Agencies

Courts

The District Court of Maryland for each county has judges appointed by the governor with consent of the state senate. This court hears cases concerning landlord and tenant disagreements and motor vehicle violations. It hears criminal cases if the sentence is less than three years in prison, the fine is less than $2,500, or both. It also hears civil cases involving penalties of up to $20,000. There are no juries in district court, so if your crime rates a jury, you must be tried in circuit court.

The District Court of Maryland for Anne Arundel County has seven judges. There are district court buildings in Annapolis and Glen Burnie. Anne Arundel County is the only county in District 7.

The District Court of Maryland for Prince George's County has eleven judges. Prince George's County is the only county in District

5. District court is held in the courthouse on Main Street in Upper Marlboro, and a district court in Hyattsville serves the upper part of the county.

The District Court of Maryland for Montgomery County has eleven judges. Montgomery County is the only county in District 6. District court is held at the District Courthouse Building at 27 Courthouse Square in Rockville.

The District Court of Maryland for Howard County has six judges. Howard County is part of District 10 along with Carroll County. District court is held in the District Court/Multi-Service Center on Courthouse Drive in Ellicott City.

The circuit court of each county is part of judicial circuits that usually include other counties. The circuit court judges are appointed by the governor with approval from the state senate. They must also get voter approval every fifteen years for continued service. Judges must retire when they are seventy years old. This court hears criminal cases, serious civil cases, and juvenile cases. It hears condemnation cases about use of land. This happens when the state needs a landowner's property to build a highway, a state park, or a state building. It also hears appeals from the district court.

Orphans' court is also part of the circuit court, hearing cases concerning wills and estates. Its judges are elected by the voters of the county.

The Circuit Court of Anne Arundel County is part of the fifth judicial circuit, which includes Anne Arundel, Carroll, and Howard counties. The circuit has seventeen judges, nine of whom serve in Anne Arundel County. Circuit court is located in the courthouse on Church Circle in Annapolis. A new courthouse began use in summer 1998.

The Circuit Court of Prince George's County is part of the seventh judicial circuit with Calvert, Charles, and St. Mary's counties. There are twenty judges. Circuit court is held in the courthouse on Main Street in Upper Marlboro.

The Circuit Court of Montgomery County is part of the sixth judicial district along with Frederick County. It has fifteen judges, who sit at the Judicial Center at 50 Courthouse Square in Rockville.

The Circuit Court of Howard County is part of the fifth judicial district with Anne Arundel and Carroll Counties. It has four judges and is held in the courthouse on Court Avenue in Ellicott City.

Law Enforcement Agencies

The Maryland State Police is a statewide law enforcement agency. Troopers have statewide jurisdiction, but generally don't enter areas patrolled by other agencies unless they are invited to do so or are pursuing a criminal. They patrol state roads and have arrangements to work with other agencies if needed. They respond to calls of vandalism, robberies, drug use, domestic violence, assaults, murders, and many other civil and criminal problems. They also patrol the roads in the counties watching for drunk drivers, reckless drivers, and speeders. Some of the troopers have dogs who work with them. The dogs are trained to sniff out drugs, and to track people who are lost or wanted by the police. There are also patrol dogs and attack dogs.

Maryland counties are also served by the MedEvac helicopter, even though there is no MedEvac station in some counties. In case of an emergency, a call is placed through the central station in Baltimore. There, a MedEvac helicopter is dispatched from one of three locations. They are Andrews Air Force Base in Prince George's County, Norwood in Montgomery County, and Martin Airport in Baltimore County. The location that is used depends on where the accident occurred and how busy the three stations are. The helicopter can be on the scene in a matter of minutes to fly out critically ill or injured people. It also helps local law enforcement agencies in rescues and in finding people who are lost or trying to evade capture.

The troopers of the Maryland State Police serve Anne Arundel County from their barracks on Taylor Avenue in Annapolis and on Aviation Boulevard in Glen Burnie, near BWI Airport.

Prince George's County has two state police barracks. One is on Rhode Island Avenue in College Park, and the other is on Forestville Road in Forestville.

The state police serve Montgomery County from their barrack in Rockville. The troopers stationed there patrol the Capital Beltway and Interstates 270 and 370, as well as other state roads in the county.

State police in Howard County serve the area from their Waterloo barrack on Washington Boulevard in Jessup.

The county police departments, like the state police, handle crime, crime prevention, and traffic control. Not all counties in Maryland have police departments. Anne Arundel, Prince George's, Montgomery, and Howard counties all have police departments.

The Anne Arundel County Police Department was established in 1937 by an act of the state legislature. Then the department had one chief, three sergeants, and seventeen patrol officers. Today the police department consists of many police officers and civilian employees who serve from the four district stations located in the county. The main headquarters building is in Millersville.

The police department in Montgomery County was first established in 1922. Policemen rode motorcycles until the 1930s, when they began to drive cars. Today the county police department has more than seven hundred officers. Five stations are located in different parts of the county. Montgomery countians are also served by park police, who patrol county-owned parks. They work their areas using cars, motorcycles, boats, and horses.

There are two police stations in Howard County. One is in Ellicott City and patrols the northern district. The other is in Laurel and patrols the southern district. The officers patrol the county, study criminal activity, enforce the laws, and handle traffic accidents. They teach citizens about personal safety and work with young people to prevent future crimes.

The sheriff is the only law enforcement officer who is mentioned in Maryland's constitution.

FUN FACT

In 1776, the Maryland Constitution established a sheriff's department in each county and Baltimore City. The sheriff was to be elected. Today the office of sheriff is still an elected one. The department works primarily with the courts. The deputies serve warrants, summonses, and other papers that are issued by the circuit court. They also have charge of transporting prisoners to court. They are responsible for the custody of the prisoners while they are at court, and they provide protection at the courthouse. The sheriff's offices also have a number of safety programs for the communities.

The sheriff's office in Anne Arundel County was started in 1650. The first sheriff was John Norwood, who was known as a shire reeve or king's man. He enforced the laws of his time, collected taxes, and served as clerk of the court. His salary was paid in tobacco. Today the sheriff's office is located in Annapolis. In Prince George's County the sheriff's office is located in the county seat of Upper Marlboro. Montgomery County's sheriff's office is in Rockville. The sheriff's department in Howard County is on Emory Street in Ellicott City.

Fire Departments

In early times, fire was a colonist's best friend and worst enemy. Fire was used for cooking, heating, and light. It could also destroy property and lives. Today fire companies are an important part of every community. They protect them from fire and other emergencies, and educate people in fire safety.

In Anne Arundel County today there are twenty-eight engine companies. There are thirteen paramedic units and eighteen basic life support units. The county also has nine truck companies and five squads. In 1995, there were 580 paid fire fighters and around 700 volunteers. Millersville is the location of the main headquarters of the Anne Arundel County Fire Department.

FUN FACT   In 1918, Severna Park established its first volunteer fire department. Its first fire engine cost $75. Today fire engines cost from $200,000 to $800,000.

In the late 1800s, towns in Prince George's County began to need fire protection. A good example of this is Hyattsville. The citizens of Hyattsville began to realize they needed a fire engine after three major fires hit their town. The last fire, which destroyed the school, many farm buildings, and livestock, prompted them to collect money to buy a fire engine. Money collected totaled $27. With that they purchased a hand pump and a barrel that were attached to a two-wheel cart. They placed a garden-type hose on the pump, and this became the very first fire engine in Hyattsville. This first fire engine was called "the Barrel."

As time passed, more towns started their own fire departments using volunteer help. Today the fire departments in Prince George's County have both volunteers and paid personnel.

Montgomery County towns began to buy fire equipment to put out the fires in the early 1800s. These early machines were hand-pulled, two-wheeled fire engines.

Today Montgomery County has seventeen fire departments and two rescue squads. There are approximately sixteen hundred fire fighters, paramedics, and emergency medical technicians, some of whom are paid and some of whom are volunteer. Seven county fire and rescue commissioners supervise the departments. A county fire board advises this commission about fire, rescue, and medical services.

In Howard County, Ellicott City's first firehouse was built in 1889, a year after the city got its first fire engine. The engine was a ladder truck that had to be pulled to the fire by the volunteer fire fighters or by a horse. Today there are eleven fire stations providing fire and rescue services to Howard County. They use volunteers and paid personnel. They promote fire safety and enforce fire codes. In addition, they provide information to the public about handling emergencies such as floods and other natural disasters.

ANNE ARUNDEL COUNTY (1650)

Anne Arundel County is unique because Maryland's capital city, Annapolis, is located there. This is where the governor lives, and where all the laws for the state of Maryland are created and passed. In addition, there are many historic buildings in the county.

By the 1990 census, there were 427,239 people living in Anne Arundel County. It is estimated that by the year 2010 there will be 511,200.

Establishment of the County

Originally, all of the land west of the Chesapeake Bay was considered St. Mary's County. Therefore, all of the land that now encompasses Anne Arundel, Prince George's, Montgomery, and Howard counties would have been included in St. Mary's County.

Anne Arundel County was established in 1650, by an act of the General Assembly of Maryland. This occurred the year after its settlement by the Puritans. It was the third county established in Maryland.

(St. Mary's was the first and Kent County, on the Eastern Shore, was the second.) The county was named in honor of Lord Baltimore's (Cecil Calvert) wife, Lady Anne Arundell, who had died the year before in 1649. She had been married to Calvert since she was thirteen, and she was only thirty-four when she died. She and Cecil Calvert had many children, one of whom, Charles, became the third Lord Baltimore. The spelling of the county name was later changed to Anne Arundel.

The county grew very fast. Soon plantations were being built to grow tobacco and other crops. These plantations were along rivers because of the ease of transportation on the water. Tobacco was generally shipped directly from these plantations, each of which had a dock.

Interesting names from some of the old homes in Anne Arundel County include Obligation, Tulip Hill, Roedown, Burrage's End, and Sur la Branche, which is French for "on the branch."

FUN FACT

County Seat

The Puritans settled at Providence in 1649, and the settlement grew so fast it expanded across the Severn River. This new area was named Anne Arundel Town, after the wife of Cecil Calvert. There were few roads at this time so Anne Arundel Town became the center of all activity. Therefore it was named the county seat in 1650, the same year the county was established. After the state capital was moved from St. Mary's City to Anne Arundel Town in 1695, the name of the town was changed to Annapolis.

Growth in the Twentieth Century

World War II permanently changed Anne Arundel County. The commission form of county government ended following the war because of the rapid growth of population. The number of people increased from 68,375 to 230,000 between 1940 and 1960. Many of the people who had moved into the county during the war decided to stay. New schools had to be built to accommodate the growing population. Older schools were remodeled. During the years after the end of World War

II, the Bay Bridge and Friendship Airport (now BWI) were built. There was an increase in businesses moving into the county, creating more jobs for the rising population. The railroad and other mass transit systems were improved and expanded to accommodate these changes.

County Government

For 136 years until 1965, Anne Arundel County was governed by a county commissioner system. No one person was in charge of the government. Instead, eight county commissioners and many independent county commissions ran the county. The Maryland General Assembly made laws according to what the county delegates and the state senator wanted. Commissioners maintained county roads and issued building permits, zoning rules, and taxicab regulations. The various commissions took care of all other functions of the county government. These included public water and sewer systems, the police department, fire companies, health, welfare, and education. County commissioners collected real estate taxes to pay for public libraries. The elected sheriff ran the county jail and served suit papers issued by the circuit court. There were so many commissioners and commissions making decisions, and so many county functions were headed by committees, that no one really knew who was in charge. As the county's population increased, it became harder for basic services to be delivered to the people.

A group of concerned citizens formed a bipartisan (combining people of different political beliefs) charter committee. They hoped to encourage voters to approve a charter form of government with a system of checks and balances to protect the public's interest. Instead of all the commissioners, they wanted a single county executive. The seven-member county council would be the legislative body. The county board of appeals, zoning hearing officer, and personnel board would become the judicial branch.

Although the new charter was controversial, county voters approved it, by a narrow margin, on November 3, 1964. Then a county executive was elected.

The county executive serves a four-year term and is limited to serving two consecutive (one after the other) terms. He or she sees to the daily operations of the county and creates the budget that is presented to the county council for its approval. Each of the seven county council members is elected to a four-year term. They meet twice a month. This charter government has remained basically the same since it was first approved by the voters.

Major Towns

Annapolis today is a bustling city with many eighteenth-century buildings. An organization called Historic Annapolis, Inc., is attempting to save many of the old buildings of the port as a reminder of the period in our history that saw the birth of our nation.

Highland Beach is the other town in the county that is incorporated. It was started in 1893 by Charles Douglass, the son of Frederick Douglass. He had been discriminated against at a resort near Annapolis and decided to start his own resort for black Anne Arundel countians. The streets are named after famous black people. Highland Beach was the first town chartered by African Americans and was incorporated in 1922. It is thought to be the first resort ever built by African Americans.

The town of Linthicum grew from the home of Thomas Lincecomb. He arrived here from England in 1658, when he was eighteen years old, and settled on the West River in southern Anne Arundel County. He acquired a great deal of land and built a plantation called Margaret's Fields. One of his grandsons, Abner Linthicum (by that time the family had changed the spelling of their name), bought land in the northern part of the county in 1801. This area is known as Linthicum Heights. Early Linthicum farmers shipped corn, wheat, and tobacco by steamship to markets in Ellicott City. Later they sold watermelon, potatoes, cabbage, and other vegetables to markets in Baltimore. With the coming of the railroad, Linthicum began to grow and become more suburban. Large corporations, such as Westinghouse, moved into the area. Friendship Airport was built there, and Linthicum became an extremely important area in the county.

The railroad was a big reason for growth in the Severna Park region also. In 1906, the Annapolis Shortline Rail Road was electrified, which shortened travel time from the area to Baltimore or Annapolis. People could live there and work in Baltimore or Annapolis. The Severn River Realty bought and developed land in the area and called it Severna

Park, although for many years, natives of the area continued to call it Boone. Boone was the name of a family of early settlers.

Glen Burnie was originally known as Tracey's Station. It became Glen Burnie in 1888, named for an estate of Judge Elias Glenn. The railroad led to its growth.

Harundale means "dale of the swallows." At one time, it was the largest housing development in northern Anne Arundel County. Its streets are named after English villages, and they are laid out in alphabetical order. This makes it easy to locate addresses.

Churches and Religion

Many of the people who came to the New World were looking for the religious freedom they did not have in Europe. After settling here, they found others with their beliefs and started churches and meetinghouses. The first church services were held in homes or outside. As soon as they could, the settlers constructed buildings for worship.

The Puritans who settled on Greenbury Point in 1649 started the first church in what would be Anne Arundel County. They worshipped in a meetinghouse on Greenbury Point. Puritans were very strict in their beliefs, following the Bible closely. They came to Maryland looking for religious freedom for themselves, but they did not want people of other beliefs to have that freedom. This led to much unrest in the colony during the following years.

Some Quakers settled in the county in the 1670s. George Fox was the founder of the Society of Friends. He arrived at the West River in 1655. He held the first meeting of Friends in April 1672 in the new Quaker meetinghouse. This is now the site of the old Quaker burying ground.

Around 1676, a group of people decided to establish a parish for the Church of England in the county. This was not accomplished until after the Protestant Revolution in England in 1689. Lord Baltimore was overthrown. Maryland became a royal colony and had a royal governor. The new governor, Lionel Copely, had the assembly pass "an act for service of Almighty God and the Establishment of the Protestant Religion in the colony." The county was divided into four parishes and churches were built for worship.

St. Anne's Parish was one of thirty established by an act of the Maryland General Assembly in 1692. In 1694, the governor proposed that a section of land be designated where a minister was to have prayers twice a day until the church building was built. It was called Middle Neck Parish, and later became St. Anne's Church in Annapolis. St. Anne's was the first brick church built in Maryland.

Today, the county is home to many religious groups including Baptist, Presbyterian, Lutheran, Catholic, Episcopal, Amish, Jewish, Jehovah's Witnesses, Methodist, and others.

The first Methodist church was located near State Circle in Annapolis. It was known as "the old blue church." It was later used as a school.

FUN FACT

Education and Schools

In early colonial times there were no schools. Children were taught at home. Older boys were sent to England, or later, to New England, to school. The first schools in the colonies started in New England.

The first schoolhouse was the Annearrundell County Free School, built around 1724. It may be the oldest schoolhouse still in existence that was established by the colonial government and paid for with public money. The school building was 25 by 18 feet, which is about the size of one classroom today. The first schoolmaster (teacher) was probably a man named John Wilmot. One of the school's most famous students, who attended from 1804 to 1807, was Johns Hopkins, who later financed Johns Hopkins University and Hospital. The Hopkins family owned a farm not far from the school.

After the Civil War, the Free School became a private home. It is now a museum.

FUN FACT

The colonial legislature encouraged people in the Maryland counties to build schools. There were twelve counties at that time. Public education in Anne Arundel County began in 1865, after the Civil War. There was no one person before that time to head a public school system. The Maryland School Law of 1865 was passed by the general assembly to ensure an education for all of Maryland's children. Reverend Libertus Van Bakkelen was the first state superintendent of schools and he worked very hard to set up an education system in Maryland. He wanted a superintendent of schools in each county, but it was a number of years before Anne Arundel County had one.

In two years, almost fifty schools were reported to have opened in Anne Arundel County. Between 1865 and 1900, the schools built were all one-room schools. The students studied reading, arithmetic, penmanship, algebra, philosophy, astronomy, and "a little French by way of recreation." Textbooks students used in their classrooms included *McGuffey's Reader*, *McGuffy's Speller*, *Brook's Arithmetic*, and *Cornell's Geography*.

FUN FACT	In the 1860s, teachers were paid $450 to $480 per year. Principals in Annapolis earned $600.

The first public high school building was Annapolis High School on Green Street. Boys were going to St. John's College in Annapolis. Eventually, people in the county saw the need for a high school for girls.

Over the next several years, superintendents (called examiners) had problems finding good teachers and problems finding enough money to run the schools. It was also difficult getting students who lived in rural areas to come to school.

After the Civil War, Maryland was slow to establish schools for black children. Some whites still did not believe black children should be educated. The Freedman's Bureau, which was established by the federal government after the war to help black people, also helped to open schools for them. However, local people did more to establish schools in Anne Arundel County than outside agencies.

In 1865, the state superintendent of education wanted schools for black children paid for by the state, just as the schools for whites were. The Maryland Assembly did not. It did, however, require counties to create funds from the taxes paid by blacks. These funds would be used to buy land on which to build freedman's schools. At that time, blacks made very little money and paid few taxes. The school fund grew slowly.

Black leaders in Annapolis opened the Stanton School in 1865. It was named after the secretary of war, Edwin Stanton. Black churches also held school. Eventually, more schools for black children were opened. It was hard to get good teachers for the black schools. Many who applied for the jobs were not well trained.

As the years passed, more schools were built. White and black children did not attend the same schools. Like the Annearrundell Free School, these were one-room schools. They were not large, most being smaller than a classroom today. The tiny schoolhouses were heated by woodstoves. In the 1930s and 1940s, consolidation (combining) of schools was begun. One-room schools began to disappear and were replaced by schools with six or seven classrooms. In 1946, the county started enlarging and remodeling older schools and building new ones. During World War II, soldiers stationed at Fort Meade arrived with their families. When the war was over, many decided to stay and call Anne Arundel County home. The need for new schools grew with the rising population.

In 1954, the U.S. Supreme Court settled a landmark (marking a turning point) case for education. In the case *Brown vs. the Board of Education of Topeka*, the court said it was unconstitutional (against the law) to have separate schools for black students and white students. All Maryland counties then began the process of desegregation, which meant that schools were open to both black and white students.

In 1997, there were more than sixty-nine thousand students in Anne Arundel County's public schools. The county also has several fine private schools serving more than thirteen thousand students. Annapolis Christian School, Key School in Annapolis, and Severn School in Severna Park are three prominent ones.

Colleges in the county are Anne Arundel Community College, north of Annapolis; the world-famous U.S. Naval Academy, also in Annapolis; University College, which is a branch of the University of Maryland; and St. John's College.

St. John's College was established in Annapolis in 1696. It grew from an earlier school called King William's School. Soldiers camped there during the American Revolution and the Civil War. It is a liberal arts college where students learn about many subjects instead of training in one specific field.

Businesses, Industries, and Agriculture

Businesses and industries are important to the growth of the counties. Anne Arundel, Prince George's, Montgomery, and Howard counties have had important businesses since colonial times. An early industry in Anne Arundel County was brickmaking, using the county's clay deposits. There were also iron ore deposits. Businesses such as the Snowden Patuxent Ironworks and the Dorsey Furnaces built furnaces to smelt (melt) the iron ore so that it could be used for building.

Annapolis was the leading import center for the colony of Maryland before the American Revolution. Maryland was importing sugar, fruit, clothing, tea, and other items not available in the colony. Its export economy was dominated by tobacco during colonial times. Tobacco was grown and shipped to Europe and other markets in huge convoys of one hundred to two hundred ships sailing together for safety.

Harvesting from the water was as important as harvesting from the land, as it is today. Oysters were harvested by skipjacks (working sailing vessels).

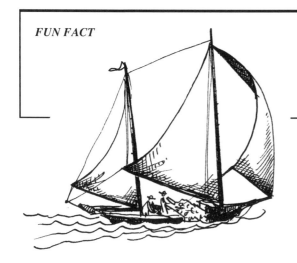

FUN FACT

Maryland still has an old law that allows only these sailing vessels to dredge for oysters (scrape them from the bottom) in the Chesapeake Bay. However, this is no longer enforced. No new skipjacks are being built because they are too expensive for watermen.

The largest employer in Anne Arundel County today is the National Security Agency, at Fort Meade. Other major businesses include Baltimore Gas and Electric, Westinghouse Electronics Systems, Computer Sciences Corporation, Giant Food,

McDonald's, Roy Rogers, and the Anne Arundel County public school system, which employs almost eight thousand people. The U.S. Naval Academy also employs many people—twenty-five hundred civilians. Many small businesses are located in shopping centers and malls around the county. The Amish community offers foods, crafts, and quilts at its Pennsylvania Dutch Farmer's Market in Annapolis.

The first McDonald's restaurant in Maryland came to Severna Park in January 1963. **FUN FACT**

The business community around BWI Airport is growing and is expected to continue to grow. Warehouse space will be extremely important. Growth of business in the county depends a great deal on the transportation network, so county planners will be looking for ways to improve an already good transportation system.

Fascinating Folks (Past and Present)

Sir Francis Nicholson is really the founder of Annapolis. He served as the Royal Governor of Maryland from 1694 to 1698. He made the decision to move the capital from St. Mary's City to Anne Arundel Town. In addition, he decided where the State House would stand, and he designed the town of Annapolis. He decided that the highest land elevation would be for public buildings. Nicholson also was responsible for the first church to be erected on Church Circle, where St. Anne's Church now stands.

Considered to be quite a swordsman, Governor Nicholson once took command of a ship and managed to defeat an entire fleet of pirates after fighting them all day on the Chesapeake Bay. **FUN FACT**

Dr. Charles Alexander Warfield was a prominent doctor in the early 1800s. He was a political leader who is said to have been the first person in Maryland to suggest that separating from England might be in the colonists' best interests. He, along with Charles Carroll of

Carrollton, persuaded Anthony Stewart to burn his ship, the *Peggy Stewart*, along with her cargo of tea.

Hogarth was a pirate who supposedly hid treasure in Anne Arundel County's Holly Hill dungeon.

Samuel Chase was one of the signers of the Declaration of Independence. Long before the American Revolution began, Samuel Chase was making speeches declaring that he "owed no allegiance to the king of Great Britain." He was instrumental in exposing a member of the Continental Congress, John Joachim Zubly, as a traitor to the colonies. The Chase-Lloyd House, still standing in Annapolis, was bought by Samuel Chase for 100 pounds of sterling silver in 1769.

FUN FACT   Because of his very red complexion, Samuel Chase's enemies called him "bacon face."

Joseph Simmons for many years rang the bell that announced the time to the townspeople of Annapolis. Because of his long, flowing hair, he was said to look like Father Time himself. Children believed they were doomed if Simmons looked at one of them and said, "I want you." Therefore, he acquired the nickname "Joe Morgue."

Aunt Lucy Smith was an African American woman famous for her cooking. She served many meals at state occasions in Annapolis.

The **Headless Man of Annapolis** supposedly haunts Annapolis, wandering along the shores, walking on the water, or walking the streets of the city. A man by the name of Thomas D. Chaney claimed to have met the headless man when he was seventeen years old. As he told the story, when he crossed a wooden bridge with loose planks, they rattled. As for the Headless Man, ". . . the man on my trail moved along with a noiseless step."

William H. Butler from Annapolis was the first black man to hold political office in Maryland. He was a Civil War veteran and real estate developer.

John Shaw was a prominent cabinetmaker for several decades in Annapolis. He built the furniture for the State House. He also made the flags with eight stars that flew in Annapolis during the time the Continental Congress met there from November 1783 through August 1784.

Johns Hopkins was born near Millersville on May 19, 1795. When he died on December 24, 1873, he left millions of dollars to establish a university and hospital in Baltimore. They are now the world-famous Johns Hopkins University and Johns Hopkins Hospital, known for having some of the finest medical research scientists and doctors in the world.

FUN FACT

Cristobol Colon was the last captive held on American soil after the Spanish-American War in 1898, but he was not a soldier. He was a parrot! Cristobol had been the parrot mascot of the Spanish cruiser *Colon*. Rescued from the burning ship by an American midshipman who planned to keep him, he was placed in a locked cage after stabbing the midshipman with his beak. Cristobol eventually landed in Annapolis. He lived for about ten more years, owned by the daughter of an officer at the Naval Academy.

Charles Wilson Peale was a famous American painter who spent most of his life in Annapolis. Besides being a painter, he also tried many other occupations such as saddler, harness maker, watch and clock tinker, silversmith, modeller, taxidermist, dentist, and lecturer. He also commanded a company of volunteers in the battles of Trenton and Germantown during the American Revolution.

Governor Thomas Bladen was the only colonial governor of Maryland who was born in America. He was born in Annapolis in 1698. Governor Bladen started the building of a governor's residence in 1744, at what is now St. John's College. This home was not completed due to lack of money.

John Boynton Philip Clayton Hill could win the prize for the longest name of anyone in this book. He was born in Annapolis in 1879.

He served as a Republican representative to the United States Congress.

Babe Phelps was born in 1908 in Odenton. He played baseball for the Chicago Cubs during the 1933–34 season and for the Brooklyn Dodgers from 1935 to 1941. He was inducted into the Shrine of Immortals by the Maryland Professional Baseball Players Association in 1969.

Charlie Byrd is a nationally known guitarist. He started his career in the 1940s. His music was influenced by a goodwill trip he once took to South America for the U.S. State Department. Since then he has been a goodwill ambassador to other countries eleven times. He is best known for bringing a style of music called the bossa nova to America from Brazil. He is still touring and performing all over the world.

Toni Braxton is a nationally known singer born in Severn. Her father is a minister and she and her five sisters grew up singing in his church. In 1997, she won two Grammy awards.

Bill Belichick is a professional football coach who grew up in Annapolis. He started his coaching career as an assistant with the Baltimore Colts, and was head coach of the Cleveland Browns for a number of years until the team moved to Baltimore to become the Baltimore Ravens.

Pat Sajak is the host of *Wheel of Fortune,* one of the most popular game shows on television. He has a home in Anne Arundel County.

Norm Lewis is the weatherman and meteorologist for WMAR-TV, Channel 2, in Baltimore. He has a home in Anne Arundel County.

There are also some authors of children's books who live in Anne Arundel County:

Priscilla Cummings is the author of the very popular *Chadwick the Crab* books. You may also have read *Oswald and the Timberdoodles* and *Sid and Sal's Famous Channel Marker Diner*. She uses environmental themes in many of her books. Cummings lives in Annapolis.

Bianca Lavies was born in Holland and lived for a time in New Zealand. She now lives in Annapolis. You may have read her books *Tree Trunk Traffic, Lily Pad Pond, A Gathering of Garter Snakes, It's an Armadillo!* and other books she has written about animals.

Richard Stack is the author of the books about Josh the Wonder Dog. Have you read *The Doggonest Vacation*, *The Doggonest Christmas*, and *The Doggonest Puppy Love*? Stack visits schools with his dog, Josh, and talks about his books.

Josh has been listed in the *Guinness Book of World Records* as the world's most petted dog. After each personal appearance, children file past Josh and pat him on the head. School principals or PTA volunteers are responsible for counting the number of pats and signing affidavits (sworn statements in writing) confirming the number.

FUN FACT

Mick Blackistone lives in southern Anne Arundel County and is the author of *The Day They Left the Bay*, *Broken Wings Will Fly*, and *The Buffalo and the River*. He has also written *Sunup to Sundown: Watermen of the Chesapeake Bay*. Blackistone speaks out about pollution and uses environmental themes in his books.

Natural Resources

Anne Arundel County's natural resources include its forests, waterways, oysters, crabs, and fish. The county has a variety of deciduous (trees that drop their leaves in the fall) and evergreen forests. Although the northern part of the county has become quite suburban, a great part of the rest of the county is still rural and covered with forests. Trees such as maple, pine, hickory, oak, and sycamore are common in Anne Arundel County's forests.

The Magothy, Severn, South, Rhode, and West Rivers are home to crabs and fish. Boaters enjoy the rivers, as do visitors to the parks located along their banks. In the past, the rivers, streams, and creeks provided power to turn mills that ground grain.

When Captain John Smith explored the Bay in 1608, he found oysters the size of dinner plates. He wrote in his journal that one oyster could make a meal for four men. Unfortunately, oysters do not get that big any more. Pollution, disease, and harvesting prevent them from reaching that size, but they are still a popular delicacy for people all over the world.

Fish such as spot, herrings, winter flounder, croakers, white perch, and striped bass (also called rockfish, or just rock) and clams are caught by sport and commercial fishermen. Some popular fish and shellfish have, at times, been at risk. During the mid-1990s, catching rockfish was prohibited because of the decline in the population of these fish. Disease killed many oysters, affecting their population.

The blue crab, found in the Chesapeake Bay and Maryland waterways, is the most popular seafood in the state. Maryland's crabs are shipped all over the world.

Places of Interest

Construction began on **Baltimore/Washington International Airport** in 1947, and it opened in 1950. It was originally called Friendship Airport because it was built in the vicinity of Friendship Church in Anne Arundel County. Present at the dedication ceremony in June 1950 were President Harry S Truman, Maryland Governor William Preston Lane, Jr., and Baltimore Mayor Thomas J. D'Alesandro, Jr.

The airport used to be owned by the city of Baltimore. In 1972, the state of Maryland bought it for $36 million through the Department of Transportation. In 1973, Friendship Airport was renamed Baltimore/Washington International Airport (BWI) because it was only 10 miles south of Baltimore and 30 miles from Washington, D.C. The airport's new name reflected its role as a transportation center for the region.

BWI has been enlarged and modernized in phases many times over the years. Its size, as of 1998, was 3,158 acres. One new feature is the two-level observation gallery. Children can enjoying playing in the make-believe airplane, baggage cart, tugboat, and fuel truck there. The second level features parts of a real Boeing 737 airplane that once was used as a charter for the Baltimore Orioles baseball team. Visitors can sit in the cockpit and pretend to be flying the plane. There are also educational exhibits, a children's play area, and a 3,000-square-foot sky window that overlooks the airfield.

BWI serves over twelve million passengers a year. There are 650 daily flights, and ten thousand people work full time at the airport.

The **William Preston Lane, Jr., Memorial Bridge,** or the Chesapeake Bay Bridge, as we call it, is one of the longest continuous over-the-water structures in the world. The first span, opened in 1952, measures 21,286 feet, or 4.03 miles. It is 28 feet wide and cost $41 million to build. Considered one of the world's most impressive bridge structures, its total length is 7.727 miles, including both approaches. At its highest point it measures 186.5 feet above the water at high tide. This is considered more than high enough to accommodate the largest ships likely to sail up the Chesapeake Bay to Baltimore.

Before the span opened, motorists wishing to cross the Chesapeake Bay had to take a state-operated ferry. This regular ferry service took two hours to make the 23-mile trip between Annapolis and Claiborne on the Eastern Shore. Ferries such as the *John M. Dennis* became obsolete with the construction of the Chesapeake Bay Bridge.

As early as 1908, engineers had studied the possibilities of building a bridge across the Bay. Finally, in 1947, under the leadership of Governor William Preston Lane, Jr., the Maryland General Assembly empowered the State Roads Commission to begin construction of the Chesapeake Bay Bridge at its present site between Sandy Point and Kent Island. Construction began in January 1949, and the bridge officially opened to traffic on July 30, 1952. In 1967, this span was rededicated and renamed the William Preston Lane, Jr., Memorial Bridge.

With traffic increasing from 1.9 million cars crossing in 1953 to 4.4 million in 1967, plans were begun for a second span. The two spans would be side by side, with the new one 450 feet north of the old one.

If this new span had been built to the south of the older one, it would have been 700 feet longer.	*FUN FACT*

Due to rising prices and higher wages, the new bridge cost $120 million to build, $79 million more than the original. It is estimated that almost eighteen million vehicles cross these two bridges annually.

The **Rising Sun Inn** is a historic tavern. Located on the Old General's Highway, a road heavily traveled during colonial times, it saw the passage of many famous people and events. A historical marker in front of the inn says that "Count De Rochambeau's troops marched over this road from Spurrier's Tavern to 'Scott's Plantation' (Belvoir) on Sept.

16, 1781 on the way to Yorktown. . . ." The inn was built by Lt. Henry Baldwin, a Revolutionary War veteran, in 1784.

The **London Town Publik House** on the South River was built between 1758 and 1764 by William Brown, who owned the South River Ferry and an inn in London Town. He was also a carpenter.

The **Anne Arundel Free School** was built in 1725 as part of the Free School Act of 1723. "Free" referred to what was taught, not to the tuition. The school was originally 25 feet by 18 feet, smaller than most classrooms today. It was enlarged in 1875 when a second story was built. The school was used until 1912, when many small schools were closed and students were sent to larger schools. The Anne Arundel County Retired Teachers Association has restored the school and it is now open to visitors as a museum.

Fort Nonsense is one of a series of forts built during the 1700s and 1800s to protect Annapolis. The forts consisted of trenches dug in the earth with embankments to make the trenches higher. Fort Nonsense was probably built after the American Revolution and was almost certainly used during the Civil War. It is now protected by federal law.

The **Thomas Point Lighthouse** was built in 1875. It is a hexagonal (six-sided), one-and-one-half story white house. It is located at the Thomas Point Shoals, a very shallow part of the Chesapeake Bay. It was originally lighted by a kerosene lamp. Now it is powered by electricity. This is the third lighthouse at this site, which can be reached only by water.

Laurel Race Course is one of Maryland's favorite horse racing tracks. It opened on October 2, 1911.

The **Historical Electronics Museum** is a great place for kids of all ages. Among its treasures is an original cylinder phonograph that still plays. There is also the video camera that went to the moon with the astronauts in 1969 and transmitted Neil Armstrong's first step on the lunar surface to televisions back on earth. The museum is located near BWI Airport in Linthicum.

Twin Oaks was to be the retirement home of Frederick Douglass. Douglass was the famous black scientist and mathematician who was chosen to help survey the boundaries of Washington, D.C. He was having this house built on the shore at Highland Beach, but he died before it was finished. It was eventually bought and restored by Charles Bohl. It is now owned by Anne Arundel County.

Jug Bay Wetlands Sanctuary is a 500-acre area of marshes, shrub land, and forest in the southern part of the county. Overseen by scientists and volunteers, its purpose is to protect natural habitats and to educate people about wetlands and their importance. If you visit Jug Bay, you may see any of more than two hundred species of birds, including eagles, and many animals and plants.

At the **Army Museum at Fort George G. Meade** visitors can see displays of events as far back as the American Revolution, as well as overseas operations in which Anne Arundel County troops were involved.

Also located at Fort Meade is the **National Security Agency** (NSA). This is an agency of the federal government dedicated to gathering intelligence information about other countries, using state-of-the-art computers and electronic equipment. It is Anne Arundel County's largest employer, providing twenty thousand jobs. It has the largest payroll, $930 million as of 1996, in the state of Maryland. Members of all four branches of the U.S. military (Army, Navy, Air Force, and Marines) work there along with civilians. Everyone must be checked by the security officers before working there, because the work is top secret. Some people decipher codes and others keep track of events in foreign countries. They use information to protect the United States and other countries in trouble. Employees can bring their children to work with them. The largest day-care center in Maryland is located there.

Some people who have worked for the National Security Agency have left for other careers. Two well-known entertainers used to work for the agency: country singer Johnny Cash and talk-show host and actor Montel Williams.

FUN FACT

NSA indirectly gives jobs to many more people than the twenty thousand who work at Fort Meade. It awards contracts to outside companies for work that adds up to hundreds of millions of dollars and thousands of jobs. The agency's economic impact on Maryland is enormous.

Places of Interest in Annapolis

The first **State House,** built in 1698, was in Anne Arundel Town. It was very small, measuring only 22 feet wide and 46 feet long. In 1704, fire destroyed the State House. It was also the courthouse, and many old records were destroyed in the fire.

The present State House, designed by Horatio Anderson, is the oldest capitol in daily use by a state legislature in the United States. It is of Georgian design, of red brick. Construction began in 1772, and was completed in 1779. The State House's wooden dome was constructed with wooden pegs only—no nails. Even today this is considered to be an architectural marvel. To get to the top of the tower, you must climb a very narrow, winding stairway of 149 steps. Security guards climb this stairway every day to put up and take down the Maryland flag.

FUN FACT	The top of the dome of the State House is also known as "the acorn" because of its shape. Since it had become rotten inside, on September 1, 1996, the acorn was lifted off by helicopter. Not long after, it was replaced by a new one, which should last several hundred years.

The Old Senate Chamber in the State House was the scene of much history in colonial times. The State House was the seat of government for the colonies for a time. The Continental Congress met there from November 1783 to August 1784.

The new Senate Chamber is where the state senate meets today. The red and white colors used in the room honor the Crossland family of George Calvert's mother. The chamber is paneled with Italian marble of black and rust colors. These colors are meant to represent the black and gold in the Maryland flag. The forty-seven senators who meet here represent the forty-seven districts of Maryland's political divisions. They meet for ninety days every year beginning in January. This room houses paintings of Maryland's four signers of the Declaration of Independence: Charles Carroll of Carrollton, William Paca, Thomas Stone, and Samuel Chase.

The House of Delegates is the meeting room for the 141 delegates. Its walls are also made of black and rust marble. The colonial delegates might have liked its current computerized voting system. Today's delegates vote with switches at their seats. Votes are recorded on a large board, which lists each legislator's name. A green light means "yea" (yes), and a red light means "nay" (no). The results of the vote appear at the top of the board and are announced by the speaker of the House.

The State House contains many interesting historic items, such as a silver service that was a gift from the citizens of Maryland, including schoolchildren. The pictures on the silver service show events in the history of Maryland and historic sites around the state. It was designed and made by Samuel Kirk and Son, Inc. In 1906, it was presented to the naval cruiser U.S.S. *Maryland*. In 1921, it was presented to the battleship U.S.S. *Maryland,* which fought in World War II. The silver service will remain at the State House until another ship is named Maryland, at which time it will be presented to her.

On December 23, 1783, General George Washington resigned as commander-in-chief of the Continental Army in the Old Senate Chamber. Washington wore no hat during the ceremony. The congressmen all wore theirs, but took them off in respect when Washington stood and bowed. A very lifelike mannequin of General Washington stands at the spot where he stood to resign his commission.

Soon after that, on January 14, 1784, the Treaty of Paris was ratified there. This officially ended the Revolutionary War.

In the State House visitors can also see a small ship, the *Federalist.* A sign by this original ship says, ". . . the *Federalist*, a 15-foot ship-rigged vessel, was built in 1788, to celebrate Maryland's ratification of the U.S. Constitution on April 28." The ship has seven sails to represent the fact that Maryland was the seventh state to ratify the Constitution.

Also on display there is a small Maryland flag that traveled to the moon on *Apollo 11,* and some small moon rocks. A plaque commemorates the space shuttle *Challenger,* which exploded shortly after its takeoff on January 28, 1986. The State House is where Maryland's newly elected governors take the oath of office every fourth year. This ceremony is rich in tradition, reflecting the proud history of Maryland.

The **Old Treasury** is located on the grounds of the State House in Annapolis. It was built between 1735 and 1737 and was used for issuing bills of credit. It is the oldest public building in Maryland.

Government House is the official residence of the governor and his family. The mansion was completed in 1870. It was built on a five-sided (pentagonal) lot.

The first governor's mansion actually used for that purpose was a house on what is now Naval Academy grounds. It was built in 1740 by Edmund Jennings, who rented it to Horatio Sharpe during Sharpe's term as governor. In 1769, the house was bought by Governor Robert Eden. Governor Eden was a royal governor and, at the outbreak of the American Revolution, he returned to England. The house was taken over by the state of Maryland and was used by governors until 1866.

A tour of the **U.S. Naval Academy** is a must for visitors to Anne Arundel County. There is a museum with model ships and historical artifacts on the grounds. Naval hero John Paul Jones is buried beneath the dome of the navy chapel. Visitors can also see the students assemble in formation between noon and 12:30.

Before the academy was established in 1845, young midshipmen learned their profession by experience. The mathematics and navigation "schoolmasters" on the large ships had difficulty teaching these young men, though, because they had no authority. Any officer could call on the midshipmen to perform duties, taking them from their studies. There were naval schools in Philadelphia, Pennsylvania, and Norfolk, Virginia, but there was very little equipment and midshipmen were frequently called to sea duty.

In 1845, the secretary of the navy, George Bancroft, suggested that all instruction be united in one school at the site of Fort Severn in Annapolis. All midshipmen on shore duty and all men wishing to qualify for positions as midshipmen would be able to study there. On October 10, with a staff of eight officers, Commander Franklin Buchanan assembled forty midshipmen who had reported to Annapolis, and started classes in naval instruction.

Subjects the midshipmen studied included arithmetic, algebra, geometry, navigation, geography, English grammar and composition, French, Spanish, trigonometry, astronomy, mechanics, optics, magnetism, electricity, ordnance (weapons), gunnery, the use of steam, history, natural philosophy, chemistry, infantry, drill, and fencing (sword fighting). The only admission requirements were some knowledge of arithmetic and geography and the ability to read and write. The entrance age was between thirteen and sixteen.

During the Civil War, the Naval Academy and St. John's College were used chiefly as hospitals for Union soldiers. Confederate prisoners were also received there. At the close of the war between the North and South, the Naval Academy returned to its quarters. Unfortunately, it had been badly wrecked by its use as a hospital. Cheap, ugly buildings had been built there for many purposes, including beer saloons.

Since the Civil War, many large, beautiful buildings have been built at the Naval Academy, such as Bancroft Hall, named after George Bancroft. Today the academy covers 338 acres.

About four thousand midshipmen and women study at the Naval Academy today, taught by more than six hundred instructors. To be accepted you must be recommended by a member of the U.S. Congress. Good grades and good citizenship in high school are very important.

The **Ghost Tour of Annapolis** is a candlelight tour at night. Visitors tour "haunted places" and hear about the ghosts and hauntings around Annapolis. Sounds like lots of spooky fun!

The **Hammond-Harwood House** is a good place to visit to see how the very wealthy lived in the 1700s. The house was designed by William Buckland and is considered to be one of America's most beautiful historic homes. It is a stop on the Ghost Tour of Annapolis because of two stories of unhappy love affairs that happened almost one hundred years apart. Do the heartbroken lovers still walk around there?

The **William Paca House and Gardens** is another good place to visit to see how the wealthy lived in the mid-1700s. The house was the home of William Paca, a signer of the Declaration of Independence who also served as a governor of Maryland. It was built between 1763 and 1765, and includes a 2-acre garden with terraces, a fish pond, and a wilderness garden.

St. John's College was the first public school built in Maryland. An act of the Maryland Assembly established it as King Williams' School. It was a grammar school and one of the free schools. The original building stood on State Circle but was torn down in 1786. In 1784, the St. John's College was chartered by an act of the assembly. The college received money and books from the former King Williams' School. The school opened in 1789. It bases its curriculum (program of subjects to study) on the Great Books program. This program involves reading and discussing books that have been considered a standard of excellence over a long period of time.

The Kunta Kinte Heritage Festival is held at the college. This festival honors the cultures and the people brought from Africa and the Caribbean to be slaves. It celebrates the arrival of Kunte Kinte, a slave from Africa whose story was told in the book *Roots* by Alex Haley.

The **Liberty Tree** on the college's campus is a tulip poplar thought to be four hundred to six hundred years old.

In 1652, a group of colonists and Susquehannock Indians smoked a peace pipe beneath the branches of the Liberty Tree. In the years before the American Revolution, the Sons of Liberty would meet there to plan action to take against British rule. By 1840, worms were gnawing away at the tree, and it was falling into decay. The tree was saved that year in a strange way. Children playing under the tree put some gunpowder in its hollow. The gunpowder caught fire and exploded. The citizens of Annapolis and firemen flooded the tree with water, and it was saved.

The fire had done a great service for the tree by destroying all the worms.

FUN FACT

No one knows its actual age, but in July 1886, the Liberty Tree measured 29 feet and 4 inches around and stood 150 feet high.

The **Banneker-Douglass Museum** was dedicated on February 24, 1984. It is housed in the Mt. Moriah A.M.E. Church on Franklin Street in Annapolis. This is one of the oldest black churches in the city. You can see African-American art, historical artifacts (handmade objects), papers, photographs, and even fossils. It is the official storage place for African-American cultural materials and artifacts in Maryland.

The **Maryland Inn** was built in stages. In 1772, Thomas Hyde had the front part of what is now the Maryland Inn constructed across the street from the State House. There have been a variety of owners over the years who have added to the building, particularly during the late eighteenth century. In the early 1900s, the inn was converted into offices and apartments. The present owners have completed its restoration. It is now once again an inn and restaurant. The restaurant is named after the Treaty of Paris, which was signed at the end of the American Revolution. The **Drummer's Lot Pub** and the **King of France Tavern** are also located there.

FUN FACT

People working on the Maryland Inn's basement discovered it had three floors and that its stone walls are 1½ feet thick.

The site of the Maryland Inn used to be known as Drummer's Lot. This was where the town drummer beat on his drum to get everyone's attention so he could tell them the latest news. The drummer used a variety of drumbeats depending on the type of news he was announcing.

This was unique to Maryland, since all other towns in the colonies used town criers. The drummers also called the state legislature to session. If, after the third roll of the drums, a state legislator was still missing, he was fined 100 pounds of tobacco.

The **City Dock** is a fun place to visit to see the many boats docked there. A long canal called Ego Alley is the heart of the dock. It is called Ego Alley because people travel up and down the alley showing off their boats. In early days, the dock was surrounded by taverns, warehouses, and a ship's carpenter's business. Today, the visitor's information booth at the dock can direct you to interesting places in Annapolis, such as the **Tobacco Prise House** near the dock, which has exhibits about the colonial tobacco trade. There is also a plaque at the dock dedicated to Kunta Kinte. Two of the largest boat shows in the world are held here: the U.S. Sailboat Show and the U.S. Powerboat Show.

Cornhill Street was one of the most important streets in Annapolis in colonial times. The streets that lead from the State House are designed to look like the spokes of a wheel. Cornhill Street was one of the first streets to form one of these spokes. In colonial times, it was one of the main thoroughfares of the town.

Parks and Recreational Areas

Sandy Point State Park is located near the Bay Bridge. Visitors can sunbathe and play on the beach, watch big ships sail up and down the Bay, go swimming and hiking, and play on the playground. Families can rent boats and go boating, or stay on land and have a picnic. This park is the site of the Maryland Seafood Festival. Chesapeake Appreciation Day is held there at the start of the Maryland oyster season and honors the watermen who work on the Bay all year. On one Sunday each May, one span of the Bay Bridge is closed to traffic, and people can park at Sandy Point State Park and walk across. The bridge is a little over 4 miles long. Do think you could walk that far?

Quiet Waters Park is located on the South River and Harness Creek. Activities at the park include hiking, bike riding, picnicking, and boating in the summer. There is a playground and, in the winter, an ice rink for ice skating.

Downs Memorial Park has biking, picnicking, nature walks, and concerts. Swimming is not allowed there. There is a youth group camp in the area. The park has 200 feet of Bay shoreline where fishing is allowed, and a small freshwater pond. The park is at Bodkin Neck, a peninsula where the Patapsco River and the Chesapeake Bay meet. The area was originally farmland. Charles Carroll of Carrollton, a signer of the Declaration of Independence, was one of the first landowners there.

Thomas Point Park is on the South River. Activities allowed there include hiking, bike riding, bird watching, and fishing, but not swimming. From the park, you can see the Thomas Point Lighthouse located offshore. The land became a park when its 44 acres were donated by Ferdinand and Jane Lee, in the early 1960s, for use as an area for recreation and conservation.

Truxton Park is on Hilltop Lane in Annapolis. The park has tennis and basketball courts, a baseball field, a swimming pool, picnic sites, and a playground. Fishing is allowed in the park.

PRINCE GEORGE'S COUNTY (1696)

Prince George's County is a gateway into the United States because diplomats and celebrities visiting Washington from all over the world land at the county's Andrews Air Force Base. The county is the home of Maryland's state university (the University of Maryland), the largest college in Maryland.

By the 1990 census, 729,268 people lived in Prince George's County. By the year 2010 it is estimated there will be 890,300.

Establishment of the County

By 1674, there were ten counties in Maryland. St. Mary's, Anne Arundel, Calvert, Charles, and Baltimore were on the western shore. Kent, Talbot, Somerset, Dorchester, and Cecil were on the eastern shore of the Bay. So many people had moved into Charles and Calvert counties that a new governmental division needed to be made for taxation and representation in the general assembly. A session of the general assembly was held on May 8, 1695, at which an act was passed dividing land that was part of Charles and Calvert counties into Prince George's. The area was established as a county in 1696, on Prince George's Day, which was April 23. Its name honors Prince George of Denmark, who was married to Princess Anne of England. Princess Anne later became queen and ruled Great Britain and Ireland from 1702 to 1714.

The new county was bigger than it is today. It included land that eventually became parts of Frederick, Montgomery, Washington, Allegany, and Garrett counties. It also included land that is now Washington, D.C.

During these early years the Protestants of the colony were angry with Charles Calvert, third Lord Baltimore. Although the Lords Baltimore allowed religious freedom in the colony, they did not allow Protestants to hold political offices. Only Catholics could hold office. (Remember, Lord Baltimore, who established the colony, was Catholic.) The Protestants rebelled against Lord Baltimore, and the colony was taken over by them. A royal governor was appointed by King William and Queen Mary. Many of the people in the area established as Prince George's County were Protestant, as were the king and queen. Historical records from that time do not make it clear whether another reason for the division was to have a Protestant county.

In 1996 and 1997, Prince George's County celebrated its three-hundredth anniversary, called a tricentennial. Events and activities throughout the year included an exhibit at the University of Maryland called "300 Candles: Slices of Prince George's County History." There were also candlelight Christmas tours of towns, a display of nineteenth-century fashions at the Surratt House in Clinton, and a display of old dolls and toys at the Montpelier Mansion in Laurel.

FUN FACT

County Seat

The first county seat of Prince George's County was Charles Town. It was established as the county seat after the Advancement of Trade Act of 1683. This act called for the building of ports and towns along the rivers and the Chesapeake Bay to trade with other colonies and other countries. One hundred acres of land on the Patuxent River were bought from William Groome for the town. A number of shops opened that sold clothing, blankets, rugs, tobacco boxes, farm tools, saddles, muskets, spices, soap, and food. Groome opened an ordinary (or inn) on his lot in town. Soon, other ordinaries and taverns were built and the town grew, but it never became very large. St. Paul's Church was also built for people belonging to the Church of England.

In June 1697, the justices of Prince George's County hired a carpenter named Robert Brothers to build a courthouse. It was finished a year later. Brothers was paid 50,000 pounds of tobacco for building the courthouse.

Prince George's County was growing very fast. By 1706, the general assembly passed another Act for the Advancement of Trade that gave locations for five new towns to be built in the county. These towns became Queen Anne, Mill Town, Nottingham, Marlborough, and Aire. (Only one of these, Marlborough, still exists today.) This was bad news for Charles Town, because these new towns took away trade. Not as many ships docked at Charles Town and people lost jobs and money. Eventually, even the ferry service was discontinued. Charles Town was a commerce center before Marlborough, but today only one building from old Charles Town still stands. It is a home called Mount Calvert.

Finally, in 1718, a group of people asked the general assembly to move the county seat from Charles Town to the Town of Marlborough. They thought Marlborough (soon renamed Upper Marlborough) was more central to the county and easier to reach. The general assembly agreed, and in March 1721, court met for the first time in Marlborough.

FUN FACT   The name Town of Marlborough was changed to Town of Upper Marlborough to distinguish it from the Town of Lower Marlborough in Calvert County. Today it is called Upper Marlboro. Both towns were named after John Churchill, the Duke of Marlborough.

The courthouse and jail in the Town of Upper Marlborough were built by Levin Covington in 1720–21. The courthouse was renovated and enlarged several times over the years.

The county continued to grow throughout the 1700s. Tobacco was grown by nearly everyone because it was used as money. People who could afford to began buying slaves so that they could grow even more tobacco, and Prince George's County began to change from a frontier area to an agricultural area.

Growth in the Twentieth Century

From about 1930 into the 1980s, Prince George's County grew very fast. The county continued the change from an agricultural to a suburban economy that had started to develop after the Civil War. The growth of the U.S. government and its many agencies created jobs and a need for houses and businesses to serve more people. The automobile and mass transit were big factors in growth. People could live in the county and commute to work in the cities of Washington or Baltimore.

Growth in Prince George's and Montgomery counties has been carefully planned over the years by the Maryland–National Capital Park and Planning Commission. This organization, which was established in 1927, oversees the development of the counties and makes sure that the parkland and open-space areas are preserved and maintained. It also purchases land for parks and recreational areas. The commission buys and preserves historic buildings, such as the Riversdale Mansion, the Surratt House, and Marietta, a house now being used as the headquarters of the Historical Society of Prince George's County. The commission also oversees planning and zoning to ensure that development in the counties does not damage the environment.

County Government

In 1798, the General Assembly of Maryland passed a law establishing election districts in all counties to replace the old "hundreds." The commissioners in Prince George's County drew the boundaries of five election districts.

Charter government was established in 1970. This government would be led by an elected county executive. The first county executive under this new charter government was William W. Gullett, who served from 1971 to 1974.

There are nine county council members who meet once a week. The council serves three functions. It handles legislative and business matters, serves as the district council on zoning and land use, and acts as a board of health to decide public health policies.

Major Towns

Bladensburg was established about 1747, when it was designated as a tobacco inspection site and port. It is remembered for the Battle of Bladensburg during the War of 1812, which did not end well for the Americans. Bladensburg today is a busy suburb of Washington, D.C.

FUN FACT   The first person in the country to send up a hot air balloon was Peter Carnes of Bladensburg, in June 1784. He sent up his balloon, which was 35 feet wide, with no one in the basket. A few weeks later, he went to Baltimore and sent up Edward Warren, age thirteen, in the first manned flight of a balloon in America.

Laurel was named after the laurel bushes that grew in great numbers in the area. In the early 1700s, a grist mill was built by Nicholas Snowden of Montpelier on the Patuxent River. In the 1820s, Snowden converted it to a cotton mill. His business grew when he added a loom to weave cloth. In 1835, the railroad came to the area and the town of Laurel grew up near the mill. Laurel's location between Baltimore and Washington was a good one and Laurel grew quickly. Today, because of its location, Laurel is the center for people living and working in all four of the Central Maryland counties.

FUN FACT   Three counties come together where a railroad bridge crosses the river at Laurel. If a train stopped in the middle of the railroad bridge, the train would be where Anne Arundel, Howard, and Prince George's counties meet. Montgomery County's line is a few miles up the river.

Hyattsville was first called Chittam's Addition to Bealle Town. It is believed that the land around this area was originally a seaport, because early settlers there who came from England and Annapolis were mariners. Hyattsville was named for Christopher Hyatt, who settled there in 1860. This city is located at the juncture of the Northeast and Northwest Branches of the Anacostia River.

Bowie was founded in 1870. At that time it was called Huntington City, but it was renamed in 1874 after Governor Oden Bowie. He served as the governor of Maryland from 1869 to 1872. The town grew up along the Pennsylvania Railroad tracks. Old buildings near the station are now antique stores.

Beltsville was named for landowner Truman Belt in 1839. It is the headquarters of the Agricultural Research Center of the U.S. Department of Agriculture which was founded in 1910. The research center covers 7,000 acres of land.

Fort Washington was named after the fort which has stood on the point between the Potomac River and Piscataway Creek since 1808.

Churches and Religion

The Church of England had established parishes in the colonies. St. Paul's Parish in Calvert County served people in the area, as did Piscataway Parish. St. Paul's Parish built a church in Charles Town, the first Prince George's County seat. It was also used as the courthouse for two years.

In 1704, there were enough people in the parish for the general assembly to divide it, and the northern part of St. Paul's became Queen Anne's Parish. Since then, many other religions have established congregations in the county.

The first Catholic church in the county, Sacred Heart-Whitemarsh in Bowie, was established in 1741. For American Catholics, it is a very historic place.

The first archbishop in America was born in Upper Marlboro in 1735. His name was John Carroll. Carroll was one of a group of men who tried without success to convince Canada to unite with the American colonies in 1776 to fight against the British.

Today there are many congregations in Prince George's County. They include Baptist, Christian, Buddhist, Brethren, Catholic, Church of Christ, Assembly of God, Apostolic, African Methodist Episcopal, Full Gospel, Episcopal, Mormon, Methodist, Islam, Jehovah's Witnesses, Lutheran, Church of the Nazarene, Hindu, Greek Orthodox, Presbyterian, Pentecostal, Seventh-Day Adventist, and many more.

Education and Schools

In colonial times, schooling was challenging for parents. Some taught their children at home. Some children were sent to schools in other counties or states, and sometimes back to England. In 1696, a county school board was established in Prince George's County. It immediately started planning the construction of schools to be paid for by export fees on products such as beef and furs, and an import tax on liquor.

After the American Revolution, district schools were built. In 1864, the government passed a law saying counties must have free public schools. Forty-three schools were built by 1865. In 1899, the first public high school was built in Laurel.

For higher education, parents had only two choices in the local area: Chestertown College in Kent County, or St. John's College in Annapolis. Some parents sent their children away to school in England or to William and Mary College in Williamsburg, Virginia.

The first school in the county established for black children was in Bladensburg. It started in 1866 in a rented building and was sponsored by the Freedman's Bureau. They hired a Quaker woman named Sallie Cadwallader to be the teacher, but local blacks protested that they wanted a black teacher. Cadwallader did become the teacher, however, and started classes in July 1866. After having a number of problems getting the school building constructed, it was finally finished in 1867. It was called the Union Institute.

Later, other schools were built to educate black children, such as the Prince George's Seminary in 1868, and soon after, the Chapel Hill School.

Most schools in the county were one-room schools, and white children and black children went to separate schools. Both of these situations changed over the years. Larger schools with several rooms were built. These were called consolidated schools. Then, in 1954, the Supreme Court ruled on the case of *Brown vs. the Board of Education* of Topeka, Kansas. The court said it was unconstitutional (against the law) to have separate schools for black students. So Prince George's County, and all the counties of Maryland, integrated (admitted both black and white students to) their schools.

Today Prince George's County has a very large public school system with many elementary, middle, and high schools. The county also has a community college located at Largo.

University of Maryland

The University of Maryland began as the Maryland Agricultural College. In 1856, Charles Benedict Calvert of the Riversdale estate, and others, decided that a college was needed to train young farmers in a scientific manner. The college they started was one of America's first agricultural colleges. It was built on part of the Riversdale estate owned by Charles Calvert. Today, this area is called College Park. Although its most important job was to teach agriculture, the students (who were all men) also received military training. Several buildings were constructed, including an administration building, classrooms, and dormitories where the students would live. At first the college grew slowly, partly because of the death of Calvert in 1864. In November 1912, several of the buildings burned. After the college was rebuilt, more courses were offered in a variety of subjects, and women could attend. In 1920, the state legislature made the college a state university.

One of the university's students came back years later to be its president. Harry Clifton Byrd served as president during the 1930s, 1940s, and early 1950s. Under his leadership the university's budget grew from $3 million to $20 million and the number of students increased as well.

FUN FACT   The football stadium at the University of Maryland is named for Byrd. In 1957, Queen Elizabeth of England visited the university and watched a football game between Maryland and the University of North Carolina played at Byrd Stadium. This game is still remembered as "the Queen's Game."

Since then, the university has continued to grow. Today there are about thirty-three thousand students at the University of Maryland. There are 350 buildings. The main campus at College Park covers 1,580 acres of land, and there are thirteen branches of the university located in other towns around the state.

Businesses, Industries, and Agriculture

After the Civil War, the tobacco industry in Prince George's County was just about wiped out. Without slaves to work in the fields, large farms could not plant the thirteen million pounds of tobacco that had been grown in the years before the war. Wheat and corn were also not grown in large quantities because of lack of workers. However, by the 1880s, more people were moving into the county. Many were farmers who had heard about land being for sale at good prices. So they moved to the county and started growing tobacco and wheat again.

Today, farmers in Prince George's County grow corn, soybeans, tobacco, and hay. They also raise horses and beef cattle.

In the past, large businesses in the county included iron smelting. Furnaces, such as those owned by the Snowden family and the

Muirkirk Furnace, were finally put out of business by the huge metal businesses in Baltimore, such as Bethlehem Steel.

Today, there are many large businesses that have their headquarters in the county and have large numbers of employees. Giant Food Corporation has its headquarters in Landover, as does Safeway. Safeway is not a locally organized company, but its distribution center for the Washington area is here. The Board of Education of Prince George's County and the University of Maryland are both large employers of county workers. The Beltsville Agricultural Research Center is another important facility. It is owned by the federal government and is part of the U.S. Department of Agriculture. Much important research has been done there to improve our food supply.

We all love to eat turkey at Thanksgiving and Christmas. Did you know that the turkeys we eat today are not like the turkeys people used to eat? After World War I, people were leaving farms and moving into cities. They often had small apartments with smaller stoves than before. Wild turkeys are long and have a high breastbone that made it difficult to fit them into the new smaller ovens. In the 1930s, the Agricultural Research Center developed a turkey with a shorter breastbone that was flat and wide. This made the turkey more round than long and easier to roast in smaller ovens. This new breed was known as the Beltsville turkey. We still eat this kind of turkey today.

There are many small businesses located in shopping centers and stores throughout the county.

Fascinating Folks (Past and Present)

Benjamin Stoddert fought with the Continental Army in the cavalry unit during the American Revolution. Twenty years later, he became the nation's first secretary of the navy.

Governor Samuel Ogle was the first man to import and breed racehorses. Today you can visit the Belair Stable Museum in Bowie. Belair is known as the cradle of American racing.

Bishop Thomas John Claggett was born October 2, 1743, near Nottingham. He was the rector of St. Paul's Parish. He was the first

Episcopal bishop of Maryland, and was the first bishop to be consecrated (appointed) in America. He also served as chaplain of the U.S. Senate for a time.

Dr. Richard Brooke was the first scientist in the county. He had two interests: the disease smallpox and the weather. He worked to develop a vaccination for smallpox. He also published his wind and temperature findings in a journal of the Royal Society of London.

"Parson" Rezin Williams was a slave on the plantation called Fairview. He is said to have written songs and hymns that were used to signal people on the Underground Railroad. Since the Underground Railroad was so secret, these songs were a safe way to communicate.

Rosalie Calvert was the wife of George Calvert of the Riversdale Plantation. She was born in Belgium and came to Maryland with her family in 1794. She is remembered for the letters she wrote to her relatives in Belgium after she married Calvert. In the letters she told of building the mansion at Riversdale and about life there as the wife of a wealthy leader in the state. The letters are now housed at Marietta, the headquarters of the Prince George's County Historical Society.

Charles Benedict Calvert was the son of George and Rosalie Calvert. He was a leader in creating the Maryland Agricultural College, the campus which is now the University of Maryland. He sold land from the Riversdale Plantation to the founders of the school.

Dr. John H. Bayne was a doctor just before the Civil War. His great love was plants and he experimented with them. He became known as "the prince of horticulture" (the science of growing plants).

Robert Bowie served three terms as governor of Maryland starting on November 14, 1803, when he was first elected.

Oden Bowie was governor of Maryland from 1869 to 1872. He was one of the founders of the Pimlico Race Course, home of the annual Preakness horserace. He also helped establish the Baltimore and Potomac Railroad through Prince George's County.

James H. Taylor was born in 1926, in Elkridge. He became a lawyer and, in 1957, opened the first black-owned law office in the state of Maryland. The office was in Fairmount Heights and was part of the Franklyn Bourne Law Offices. In 1963, he became an assistant state's attorney, and in 1969, he became the first black circuit court judge of Prince George's County. He was also the first black person to be elected to the Democratic State Central Committee.

The ancestors of **Nellie Plummer** were slaves who lived on the Riversdale Plantation before the Civil War. In 1927, she published a book about her family history. It was based on a diary her father, Adam Plummer, had kept while he was a slave. The book is called *Out of the Depths*.

John W. Greene, Jr., started the first black-owned airport in the county in 1941. He was born in Chattanooga, Tennessee, in 1901. In 1940, he and a group of people started a flying club called the Cloud Club. Then they decided to establish their own airfield. They rented a field and built an office, a small hangar, and a large hangar. The new airfield's flight school was used by the navy during World War II. The airfield is now closed.

In 1964, **Vera F. Rollo** founded the Maryland Historical Press, which publishes books about Maryland and other subjects. She has also written many books about the history, famous people, and government of Maryland. She is a pilot and has written books and articles about aviation.

Mary Downing Hahn is the author of books for young people, such as *Daphne's Book*, *Time for Andrew*, *Stepping on the Cracks*, and *The Wind Blows Backwards*. She was formerly a children's librarian with the Prince George's County Public Library, and now writes and speaks to schools and organizations.

Riddick Bowe was born in 1967 in Brooklyn, New York. He now lives in Fort Washington, Maryland. His boxing career has won him four Golden Glove awards and a silver medal at the 1988 Olympic Games in Seoul, South Korea. He was heavyweight champion of the world in 1992–93, and in 1993 was awarded the Jim Thorpe Pro Sports Award.

Brady Anderson plays on the Baltimore Orioles baseball team (number 9). He was born in Silver Spring on January 18, 1964. He bats and throws left-handed. He has been rotated between playing left and center field. He is also an exceptionally good batter.

Natural Resources

Although Prince George's County does not have a wide variety of major natural resources, sand and gravel are mined for use in the construction industry. The Potomac River, streams, and wooded areas are vital natural resources for recreation and quality of life.

Places of Interest

Andrews Air Force Base was established in 1942 by President Franklin D. Roosevelt. It was used at that time for Army pilot training and for air defense during World War II. Today it is used as a port of entry for foreign officials, both governmental and military, arriving in the United States. In addition, religious leaders, such as the Pope, are welcomed there.

The air base covers 7,809 acres, and more than six thousand people work there. The Naval Air Facility has a base at Andrews, as do the D.C. Air National Guard and the U.S. Air Force and Marine reserve units.

The **NASA/Goddard Space Flight Center** is an internationally known facility for tracking and collecting information from satellites and other spacecraft such as the Hubble Telescope. It was established in 1959 and named after Dr. Robert Goddard, who invented the liquid-fuel rocket. The Goddard Center was the first facility ever built for NASA (the National Aeronautics and Space Administration). Scientists and engineers design, develop, and build satellites to orbit the Earth and gather information, such as weather data.

The center is a great place to learn about America's space flight program. There are many rockets, both real ones and models, to see. Model rocket launches are held on the first and third Sundays of every month.

The **College Park Airport Museum** is the world's oldest continually operated airport. It was built by none other than Wilbur and Orville Wright in 1909. They taught two army officers to fly their "aeroplane," making it the first military airplane sanctioned (approved of) by the U.S. government. You can see displays with uniforms, airplane models, and old photographs.

This airport is extremely important in aviation history. There were many "firsts" here: the first military officer to fly a plane owned by the government in 1909, the first woman passenger in an airplane in 1909, the first testing of a bomb being dropped from an airplane in 1911, the first U.S. Air Mail service in 1918, and the first helicopter flight in 1924.

FUN FACT

Merkle Wildlife Sanctuary near Upper Marlboro is a breeding and nesting ground for Canada geese. It was established in 1932. There is a visitor's center where you can learn all about the geese and other wildlife in the county.

Fort Washington National Park houses the fort with its cannons and drawbridge. The fort was built between 1814 and 1824. There was an earlier fort at the same location called Fort Warburton. Fort Washington was built to protect the city of Washington from the British during the War of 1812.

The **Surratt House** is the place where John Wilkes Booth and his fellow conspirators met and planned the assassination of President Lincoln and others. The house was used as an inn, a post office, a tavern, and a polling place. During the Civil War, it was used to hide Confederate sympathizers from the Union Army. Visitors can see the house as it was during that time and go up to the attic to see where they hid guns.

The National Colonial Farm was established in 1958 by the Accokeek Foundation. Visitors can see what life was like in the 1700s on a colonial farm. It is located on the Potomac River in Accokeek.

Darnell's Chance in Upper Marlboro is also known as Buck House. This house is thought to be the birthplace of John Carroll, who was the first bishop of the Catholic Church in America. It was built between 1694 and 1713 by Colonel Henry Darnell, a relative of the Calverts.

Marietta is a farm in Glenn Dale dating from the 1800s. It is now the headquarters of the Prince George's County Historical Society. Old pictures, maps, and other exhibits help visitors understand what life was like in the past. Each year the historical society holds events for kids, such as a games day (playing old games from the past), a history project competition, and a Mad Hatter's Tea Party. Marietta was the home of Gabriel Duvall, an associate justice of the U.S. Supreme Court. The grounds include his law office and root cellar where food was stored. There are also beautiful old trees on the grounds. Three of them are pecan trees grown from seeds given to Judge Duvall by his friend Thomas Jefferson.

Riversdale was the home of George Calvert and his wife, Rosalie. The mansion was started by Rosalie's father and brother, but they returned to their home in Belgium before the house was finished. So Rosalie and George finished it and lived there. It was the location of many historic events, such as experimentation with the telegraph, and the beginnings of the college that became the University of Maryland. Today the mansion is open to the public.

The **National Wildlife Visitor's Center** is a large science and environmental center located in Laurel and run by the Department of the Interior, an agency of the U.S. government. It educates its visitors about the earth's resources. There are exhibits about bird migrations, endangered species, and many other fascinating things. Visitors can also learn about the scientists who are working to save wildlife and their habitats.

The **U.S. Air Arena** in Largo used to be known as the Capital Center. It is the home of the NHL's (National Hockey League) Washington

Capitals, the NBA's (National Basketball Association) Washington Wizards (formerly the Washington Bullets), and Georgetown University's Hoyas basketball team. There are also many concerts and other events held there during the year.

The **Paul E. Garber Restoration Facility** in Suitland is owned by the Smithsonian Institution. Old airplanes and space vehicles are restored and preserved here.

The **Belair Mansion** is located in Bowie. The oldest part was built around 1745. Many governors have lived there, as has William Woodward, a famous owner of racehorses. The mansion is open to visitors. You can see the **Belair Stable** there. The stable has housed such famous horses as Gallant Fox, Omaha, and Nashua. The stable was closed in 1957. At that time, it was the oldest continually operating stable for racehorses in the United States. It has been restored and is open as a museum.

The **Huntington Railroad Museum** in Bowie was the first station built by the Baltimore and Potomac Railroad Company, in 1872. The town grew up around this station, which was in service until 1989. It has been restored and is open to visitors.

FUN FACT

Back in the 1700s and early 1800s, when men were mining for iron ore between Washington, D.C., and Baltimore, a fascinating discovery was made. These men found so many Cretaceous period dinosaur fossils that the area was then called **"Dinosaur Alley."** Since then many other fossils have been found. One was a tooth from a young tenontosaur. Another was a 4-foot-long dinosaur leg bone, which is now on display at the Smithsonian Institution in Washington, D.C. Other dinosaur leg bones as well as toe bones and ribs have been found. Such a large variety of dinosaur bones has been found on the grounds of the Maryland Clay Products Company, in the Beltsville area, that paleontologists (scientists who study fossils) expect to find more in the future.

Parks and Recreational Areas

Adventure World near Mitchellville is a large theme park that is very popular with families from up and down the East Coast. Its roller coaster is the biggest in Maryland.

Rosaryville State Park is a 998-acre park near Clinton. It is located on the Mt. Airy Plantation, which was built in the mid-1700s by the Calvert family. Visitors can fish and walk the scenic trails.

Patuxent River Park is a beautiful park along the river. People take nature tours, go hiking, and picnic by the river.

Greenbelt Park is located south of Greenbelt. It consists of 1,176 acres. Visitors can enjoy camping, nature trails, and horseback riding. The Baltimore Washington Parkway cuts through the middle of it.

Piscataway Park lies along the Potomac River. George Washington is said to have enjoyed overlooking this land from his home at Mt. Vernon. It covers 1,091 acres between Mookley Point and Marshall Hall.

Watkins Regional Park on Route 556 was originally a dairy farm. The Maryland–National Capital Parks and Planning Commission turned it into a park with a children's zoo, a miniature train, a farm, and a nature center. Visitors can picnic and play tennis.

CHAPTER 10

MONTGOMERY COUNTY (1776)

Montgomery County was born the same year as our country, 1776. While patriots were planning the war for independence from England, Montgomery County was being divided from the lower Frederick area.

By the 1990 census, Montgomery County had a population of 757,027 people. It is estimated that by the year 2010, there will be 945,000.

Establishment of the County

Montgomery County was established in 1776 and was at first called Lower Frederick County. It was one of the three parts of the original Frederick County. This whole area was settled by Germans who migrated from Philadelphia. In 1776, the population of the area had become quite large, so the Frederick area was divided into three parts. The central part remained Frederick County. The western part became Washington County. And the southern section became known as Lower Frederick County. In 1778, this section was renamed for Richard

Montgomery, who was a general in the Continental Army. Because of his desire to help the colonists in their fight for liberty and freedom from England, he became a symbol of the Revolution to them.

FUN FACT   General Montgomery was born in Ireland and never spent a minute in the county that was named for him. In fact, he was dead by the time Montgomery County was established. The county was the first one in Maryland named after someone other than a European prince, duke, or lord. It was the first county in the United States to be named after a high-ranking officer who died in the American Revolution.

County Seat

Rockville is the county seat of Montgomery County. It is the second largest city in the county. Rockville was originally known as Hungerford's Tavern, after a colonial tavern located there. The tavern was an important site of planning meetings before and during the American Revolution. It was at this tavern that the Frederick County, Maryland Resolutions were written.

The town of Rockville was selected as the county seat of Montgomery County in 1777. The courthouse was built soon afterward, and court was held beginning in 1779. In 1784, William Prather Williams bought land around the courthouse, laid out streets and lots, and decided to call it Williamsburg. In 1798, five election districts were established and, in 1799, the first commissioners were appointed. In 1803, the commissioners had the town surveyed and planned. They renamed it Rockville, after nearby Rock Creek. The town was incorporated as a city in 1860.

Growth in the Twentieth Century

Montgomery County has grown tremendously since the turn of the century. In 1900, there were only about 30,000 people living in the county. Today there are more than 785,000. This growth is due to the county's closeness to Washington, D.C., with its many government agencies that employ thousands of workers. The Civil Service, started in 1893, opened the door for these jobs. The county also grew quickly because of the rail and trolley service that allowed people to live in the county and get to work in the city with relative ease. Eventually, many people began driving cars instead of depending on the trains and trolleys.

The great growth in population has changed the look of Montgomery County. Many farms have disappeared and the land is now used for housing developments or shopping centers.

County Government

Montgomery County was the first county in Maryland to adopt a charter form of government, in 1948. Before 1948, all laws were passed in Annapolis. People did not feel that they had a say in their government. Montgomery's charter government includes a county executive and a nine-member county council to run the county. Members are elected every four years. The council sets tax rates, passes legislation, and adopts the budgets for both the county and the school system. Five members are elected by separate districts and four are elected by the whole county.

Other elected positions are those of judges, the clerk of circuit court, the register of wills, the state's attorney, and the sheriff.

Montgomery County residents have seven senators and twenty-one delegates who represent them in the Maryland General Assembly.

Major Towns

There are twenty-three cities and towns in Montgomery County. The major towns include Rockville, Bethesda, Chevy Chase, Gaithersburg, Silver Spring, Takoma Park, and Wheaton.

FUN FACT

Silver Spring gets its name from a now dried-up spring that had sparkling pieces of mica (a mineral) on the bottom. The spring dried up in the 1950s, and its site was recently confirmed by local historians. There is a forty-year-old fountain at the site. The town started as a suburb of Washington, D.C., around the year 1918.

Takoma Park was originally located in Prince George's County, Montgomery County, and Washington, D.C. It is now considered to be entirely in Montgomery. Takoma has various translations in Indian language. One is "close to heaven," another is "exalted," and another is "high place." It is not known from which Indian language this came.

Wheaton is named for Civil War General Frank Wheaton.

Bethesda means "house of mercy" in Hebrew. In the early 1800s, this town rose up around a store and the tollhouse on the Washington and Rockville Turnpike. Bethesda was first called Dorsey, which was the name of the store owner. Eventually the name was changed to Bethesda after a Presbyterian meetinghouse nearby.

Chevy Chase is one of the first planned communities in the county. Because Chevy Chase and the town of Bethesda are so close to Washington, D.C., they have been nicknamed "Uptown Washington." The original spelling of Chevy Chase was "Cheivy Chace."

Gaithersburg has had several names over the years. One was Log Town and another was Forest Oak after an old, very large tree in the town. Gaithersburg was established in 1878, and is known as the heart of Montgomery County. There you can find the J. A. Building/Olde Towne Tavern and Brewing Company. This is Montgomery County's oldest business. It was built in 1903 as a general store, post office, and town meeting hall.

Rockville has had several names over the years. For a while it was called Own's Ordinary. By 1774, it was being called Hungerford's Tavern, after the tavern there. Then it became Montgomery County Courthouse, then Williamsburg, and finally Rockville. The town originally had six streets.

Although not a large town, Garrett Park is interesting because the entire town is registered as a historic district. This is unique since usually only parts of towns are designated as historical districts.

Churches and Religion

Montgomery County's first church was Rock Creek Chapel, built in 1739. It was the church for Prince George's Parish. In 1808, the congregation built a larger church, and renamed the original Christ Church. A third church was built at its present location in Rockville in 1821. The original site is still used as the cemetery for this church. It is also within the town boundary of Rockville.

Two early Catholic churches were built in the county. One was established by John Carroll in 1774, near the town of Forest Glen. He was also the first pastor of the church and, in 1784, he was appointed head of the Catholic Church in Maryland. A replica of this church is now on the grounds of Forest Glen Church.

Members of St. Mary's Catholic Church and the Shrine of Our Lady of Fatima built a church in Barnesville in 1769. The church burned down three times. The present church was built in 1900 on the same site.

People who died of yellow fever while building the Chesapeake and Ohio Canal are buried in this churchyard in Barnesville.

NOT-SO-FUN FACT

The Presbyterian Church was organized in 1649, at the area known as Cabin John. Reverend James Hunt was its first pastor and he also ran a school on Bell's Mill Road. The first Methodist church was established by Robert Strawbridge at Goshen near Latonsville. The earliest record of this church dates back to 1778.

Other historic churches in the county are St. John's Episcopal Church in Olney (the oldest Episcopal church in continuous use in the county), St. John the Evangelist Catholic Church in Silver Spring, and the Quaker Meetinghouse in Sandy Spring.

Today in Montgomery County there are churches of many different faiths, including Presbyterian, Buddhist, Lutheran, Methodist, Hindu, A.M.E. Zion, Episcopal, Catholic, Baha'i, Seventh-Day Adventist, and Baptist.

Education and Schools

Early schools taught a very basic education. Children of wealthy families were taught at home by parents or by tutors. Some sent their children to schools in Frederick or Georgetown. The first school that could give students a higher education was started by the Reverend James Hunt toward the end of the Revolutionary War. He opened the school on his farm, which was called Tusculum. The school closed when Hunt died in 1793. In 1805, parents asked the General Assembly of Maryland to help them to build a school. The general assembly gave them permission to hold a lottery to earn $2,500. This was to be used to build a schoolhouse and to buy a fire engine. The school, called the Rockville Academy, was finished in 1812. The first principal was Reverend John Brackenridge, a Presbyterian minister from Pennsylvania. Students attended until 1920. The Rockville Academy building is still in existence, and is being used as an office building. Another school built about the same time was the Brookeville Academy, in 1814. Other early Montgomery County schools were Seneca Schoolhouse (1863), the Kingsley Schoolhouse (1893), and Poole's Tract (1879).

From early days until the 1920s, most schools were one-room schoolhouses. Black students and white students attended separate schools.

FUN FACT

It was during the 1920s that the first school bus in the county began taking children to school. It was a carriage pulled by two horses. This is believed to have been the first school bus in the state of Maryland.

Desegregation of Montgomery County schools was done one school at a time. It started after the Supreme Court ruled, in 1954, that separate schools for black and white students were unconstitutional (against the law).

Today Montgomery County has the third largest school system in the state and is rated among the best in the United States. There are seven members on the school board, whose job it is to run the school system.

There are also many fine private and parochial (connected with a church) schools in the county, including several Montessori schools, the Stephen Knolls School in Kensington, the Karma Academy in Rockville, and the Muslim Nursery Kindergarten in Takoma Park.

Several colleges are located in the county. Montgomery College has campuses in Takoma Park, Germantown, and Rockville. It began as a junior college in 1946. In 1969, the name was changed to Montgomery College. It is a two-year community college.

Other schools, such as the University of Maryland, Johns Hopkins University, Hood College, and George Washington University, hold classes in Montgomery County.

Businesses, Industries, and Agriculture

Because it is so close to Washington, D.C., Montgomery County has many businesses that provide services to the U.S. government. One of these, GTE Government Systems, is recognized as a leader in many aspects of communication and electrical products. It is the largest telephone exchange company in the United States.

Another interesting company in Montgomery County is the Gillette Company. King Camp Gillette started the Gillette Company in Boston in 1904. Gillette came up with the idea of having a razor with a replaceable blade. It was called the safety razor.

Other large, important companies in the county include IBM in Gaithersburg, COMSTAT in Clarksburg, and ANT Telecommunications, Inc., in Gaithersburg. Another large employer is the Montgomery County school system.

There are also many small businesses throughout the county and in malls and shopping centers.

Farming has been important in Montgomery County for hundreds of years. In the 1700s tobacco was the leading crop. County farmers formed a group known as the Sandy Spring Farmers Society to encourage "scientific farming." The farmers originated the first agricultural fair and the first agricultural magazine in the United States to encourage farming. Growing wheat became the most popular farming activity in the 1800s, followed by dairy farming in the 1900s.

Fascinating Folks (Past and Present)

Josiah Henson was a slave on the Riley plantation located near Rockville. He was considered by his master to be trustworthy and was allowed to go into Washington to sell produce. He also became a preacher. He eventually escaped to Canada.

FUN FACT   Henson is now remembered as the model for Uncle Tom in the book *Uncle Tom's Cabin,* by Harriet Beecher Stowe. The house where he is thought to have lived is still standing just south of Rockville. It is called Uncle Tom's Cabin and is now a private home.

Martha Purdy Butler was a slave whose story was told by Josiah Henson in his recollections of slavery.

Noah Edward Clarke spent most of his adult life working to improve education for black children in the early 1900s.

FUN FACT   As a young student in school, Clark played many musical instruments, including the accordion, violin, harmonica, mandolin, organ, guitar, piano, and alto horn.

Thomas Moore was a Quaker who invented a box to keep dairy products cool as they were being shipped to market. At first it was called an icebox. He eventually renamed it a refrigerator.

In the early 1800s **Benjamin Henry Latrobe** drew many sketches and watercolors of Montgomery County. He did this to record the day-to-day life of people in the early towns. Thanks to him, we know what these towns looked like long ago. He is best known, however, for his architecture, and is called the father of American architecture. Latrobe is most famous for his work on the Capitol in Washington, D.C., and on the Basilica Cathedral in Baltimore.

One of Montgomery County's most famous citizens was **Clara Barton**, the founder of the American Red Cross. Barton was born on December 25, 1821, in North Oxford, Massachusetts. Her full name was Clarissa Harlow Barton. Because she was such a small person, her father told her she should be a schoolteacher. Barton did teach for a while, but stopped and moved to Washington, D.C. At that time it was unusual for an unmarried woman to move away from home.

During the Civil War, Barton worked for the Union cause. She advertised in Massachusetts newspapers for supplies to nurse wounded soldiers. She became known as "the angel of the battlefield," because she would carry supplies and nurse wounded soldiers on the battlefields. After the war, she started an organization that searched for men missing in the war. The group identified and marked more than twelve thousand graves in the Andersonville National Cemetery in Georgia.

Between 1869 and 1873, Barton spent time in Europe, where she learned about the International Red Cross, an organization that had been started over there. When she came home, she tried to convince people of the need for a similiar group here.

In May 1881, she organized the American Red Cross and was chosen as its first president. She served as president from 1882 to 1904.

Clara Barton realized that the Red Cross could be useful to private citizens as well as soldiers. Today, its members respond to victims of floods, hurricanes, fires, and other catastrophes in this country and others. They continue to aid military personnel in combat.

Barton's house in Montgomery County is where she lived until her death in 1912. The house is in Glen Echo and is open to the public. It is named Red Cross.

After living through the American Revolution, **Isaac Briggs** (1763–1825) worked very hard to improve our country. He was a bank president, but he was also recognized for his knowledge of astronomy, geometry, science, and mathematics. He engineered many projects, such as the Erie Canal in New York.

Francis Scott Key Fitzgerald was a famous novelist who wrote *The Great Gatsby* and *The Last Tycoon*. At his death on December 21, 1940, he was buried in Rockville near his family home. He was a member of the famous Key family. He is better known as F. Scott Fitzgerald.

Henry Blair invented a machine called a seed planter. It combined plowing and sowing the seeds into one machine pulled by a horse. He was the first African-American to get a patent from the U.S. Patent Office. This meant that only Blair could make, use, or sell his invention.

Commander E. Brooke Lee distinguished himself by leading the 115th Infantry in World War I, which earned him the Distinguished Service Cross and other citations. He was still in command during World War II.

Rachel Carson was a marine biologist and writer of books about science. Her books stressed ecology and the interdependence of man and all other living things. Her most famous book was *The Silent Spring*. She was born in Springdale, Pennsylvania, but lived a good part of her life in Silver Spring.

Walter Perry Johnson was one of the five original members of baseball's Hall of Fame. He signed a contract in 1907 with the Washington Senators baseball team. His greatest achievement was pitching three consecutive shutout games (the other team did not score) against the New York Yankees. He settled in Montgomery County after retiring from baseball in 1936 and became a farmer. He was elected Montgomery County commissioner in 1938. A high school in Bethesda is named after him, as is Walter Johnson Road in Germantown.

Sugar Ray Leonard, nicknamed after boxing champion Sugar Ray Robinson, was born Ray Charles Leonard in 1956 in Wilmington, North Carolina. He became famous when he won the gold medal in the light welterweight competition of the 1976 Summer Olympics. Since then, titles he has won include World Boxing Council Welterweight in 1979, World Boxing Association Junior Middleweight Champion in 1981, and World Boxing Council Middleweight in 1987. He won his last two titles in 1988, in super middleweight and light heavyweight bouts (matches). He now lives in Potomac.

Goldie Hawn was born in Takoma Park in 1945. She has starred in movies such as *Cactus Flower,* for which she won an Academy Award for best supporting actress. She was nominated as best actress for *Private Benjamin*. Hawn now lives in California where she owns a production company and makes movies.

Annette Klaus writes books for young readers, including *Alien Secrets* and *Silver Kiss*.

Natural Resources

Between 1900 and 1940, gold was discovered and mined at several places in Montgomery County. The mines closed eventually because not enough gold was found for the mines to be a success. Red sandstone is also found in the county, and was used in building some of the earlier museums of the Smithsonian Institution in Washington, D.C.

The Potomac River with its Great Falls is considered Montgomery County's greatest natural resource. There is a concentration of rare plants and mosses in the area of the Great Falls, due to the rocks and rushing water that create a natural habitat for them.

There are streams, forests, and river islands in the county that provide additional habitats for plants and wildlife. They also give people a place to go for recreation. Today, however, the county is very metropolitan (many buildings with few natural areas remaining). The county considers its remaining natural areas so important that they have established nature centers in Rockville, Bethesda, Boyds, and Wheaton. There are 37 miles of trails on which hikers can enjoy the county's beauty. The county also has a number of lakes that are open for fishing.

Because of the large amount of building in the county, there has been a huge decline in songbirds. An organization called Partners in Flight is attempting to lure the songbirds back.

Places of Interest

Since the roads were so bad at the beginning of the nineteenth century, county leaders looked for better transportation routes and decided to build a water highway. They called it the **C&O (Chesapeake and Ohio) Canal.** The planners designed the canal to run along the Potomac River. Work was begun on the canal in 1828. The first shovelful of dirt was dug by President John Quincy Adams on July 4, 1828. On the same day work was begun on the Baltimore and Ohio Railroad, with the same goal of making transportation west easier. These two companies became bitter enemies because each wanted people to use their service to travel west.

The canal was never completed all the way to Ohio because the railroad was a faster way to travel and could carry more freight and passengers. The canal only reached as far as Cumberland, and it took eight years to build it that far. Thirty-seven miles of the canal run through Montgomery County. This part was finished in 1833. The canal helped farmers because it created a new way for them to ship produce to more markets. Waterfalls on the canal powered mills along its banks.

By the 1950s, the canal was no longer used to carry produce. Plans were being made to bulldoze the canal and pave it as a highway. These plans were changed by the efforts of Supreme Court Justice William O. Douglas. He convinced those who wanted to bulldoze the canal to walk with him its entire length. He hoped to show them the canal's historical, cultural, geological, and botanical importance. In 1954, they took that walk with him and were convinced the canal should not be destroyed.

The **Beall-Dawson House and Stonestreet Medical Museum** is now the Montgomery County Historical Society. It is said that several ghosts have been seen there. One of them is a black man, Nathan Briggs, who worked on many renovations to the building. Other strange happenings have also occurred there, including unusual sounds floating through the house and burglar alarms that go off when no intruder is in the house. Dr. and Mrs. Paul Bryon, who used to live there, claim a ghost climbed the stairs, walked around, and even played the piano.

Needwood Mansion is now owned by the Maryland–National Capital Park and Planning Commission. It is said to be haunted by the ghost of William George Robertson, a former owner. Employees working in this building have found doors that open and close by themselves, have heard footsteps in empty offices, and have heard crashing noises and seen flickering lights. It is said Robertson began to haunt the building after he was struck and killed by lightning at the gate to his house.

The **Old Goshen Methodist Church** is known for its ghost who dressed up one evening like a preacher. He held his hands up in front of him to stop the traffic going by the church.

St. Mary's Church Cemetery, the burial place of F. Scott and Zelda Fitzgerald, is located in Rockville.

The **Boyds Negro School House** in the town of Boyds is a restored one-room schoolhouse that opened in 1896 and closed in 1936. It is now open to the public by appointment.

Clara Barton National Historic Site is located in Glen Echo. It was built in 1891 and was the home of Clara Barton, the founder of the American Red Cross.

Glen Echo Park Historic District is located in Glen Echo next to the Clara Barton Historic Site. This park used to be an amusement park with a swimming pool that could hold three thousand people. The pool and the amusement park are now closed, and the site houses an arts center. One attraction is the Dentzel Carousel, built in 1921, which has fifty-two hand-carved animals on it. The carousel is still operational and is used sometimes, though not as often as when the park was an amusement park. Today people can watch artists while they work, and can attend two children's theaters. One of them is The Puppet Company Playhouse, which performs a different puppet show each month.

Chesapeake and Ohio (C&O) Canal National Historic Park in Potomac was established in 1830. A hiking and biking trail runs for 185 miles along the canal. For extra fun, a mule-drawn canal boat ride leaves from Georgetown or Great Falls. At the Olmstead Bridges there is a great view of the falls on the Potomac River.

National Capital Trolley Museum is located just north of Wheaton. Twenty-minute rides are offered on antique streetcars from the United States and Europe.

The spires of the **Washington Temple** in Kensington can be seen from the Washington Beltway. They look like the roof of a fairy-tale castle. This is the Mormon Temple. Although only Mormons can enter the temple, there is a visitor's center with exhibits and films about how the temple was built. A good time to go is at Christmas for the Festival of Lights. The Festival of Lights includes three hundred thousand lights and a live nativity scene.

White's Ferry, in Dickerson, began service in 1828. This is the only ferry still operating on the Potomac River.

The **Seneca Schoolhouse Museum** in Poolesville shows what it was like to go to school in the 1800s.

Parks and Recreational Areas

Great Seneca Park and **Seneca Creek State Park** are two large parks that, combined, run the entire length of the county. Seneca Creek State

Park has a 90-acre lake. Adults can enjoy a game of golf. There are many historic mills and stone quarries. Hiking, biking, fishing, a playground, canoeing, and shopping at the gift shop are also available to visitors.

Patuxent River State Park offers hiking, fishing, and nature trails for walking or riding horses.

Meadowside Nature Center is in Rockville. It has 8 miles of nature trails, a lake, hummingbird and butterfly gardens, and many hands-on exhibits and displays. There is also a raptor (bird of prey) aviary (a space in which to keep birds).

Wheaton Regional Park has ice skating, horseback riding, ball fields, tennis, a carousel, train rides, and campgrounds.

Great Falls Recreational Area on the Potomac River is appropriately named because the water rushes over many rocks, creating hundreds of falls. The Chesapeake and Ohio Canal follows the river. This is considered some of the most beautiful scenery in Maryland.

Cabin John Park covers 548 acres of land on which there are ball fields, tennis courts, an ice skating rink, and other sporting areas. There are also a playground, a train ride, and a picnic area.

CHAPTER 11

HOWARD COUNTY (1851)

Traveling through Howard County is like being in a time machine. Visitors to Ellicott City can see one of Maryland's oldest towns, while ten minutes away is one of its most modern cities, Columbia.

By the 1990 census, there were 187,328 people living in Howard County. It is estimated that by the year 2010 there will be 288,700.

Establishment of the County

In 1659, the General Assembly of Maryland made Howard County part of Baltimore County. It remained in Baltimore County until 1726, when it was returned to Anne Arundel County. It was known as the Howard District of Anne Arundel County from 1839 until 1851. In 1852 it was established as a separate county. The new county was named after soldier and statesman John Eager Howard, who was the fifth governor of Maryland.

County Seat

Ellicott's Mills was the logical town to be the Howard County seat. Not only did the railroad come to the town, the Western Turnpike from Baltimore to Frederick passed through the town. There were many mills and other businesses in the area.

Once the county was established, county commissioners began to run the county as early as 1847. It is not known whether they were appointed or elected. The first commissioners were Theodore Tubman, Charles R. Simpson, William Hughes, John Hood, and George Howard. The county court was started in 1851. When this occurred, lawyers moved to the town, adding to its growth. The county commissioners met regularly, overseeing roads, schools, and other county business.

In 1867, a city charter was granted by the Maryland General Assembly, and the town's name was changed from Ellicott's Mills to Ellicott City. It is still called Ellicott City, although it no longer has its charter. Local people had protested taxes on real estate and asked that the charter be repealed (stopped). The general assembly agreed and took back the charter in 1935. Even today, Howard County has no incorporated towns.

Growth in the Twentieth Century

During the years since World War II, Howard County has grown faster than at any other time in its history. Many professional people such as lawyers, accountants, and doctors have found Howard County's rural beauty to their liking. People agreed that they did not want too much growth. They wanted the county to remain mostly rural. However, new services were needed for the growing number of people, and so shopping centers, libraries, newspapers, and the YMCA came to the county. New schools were built and new businesses opened. The event that had the greatest impact on the county occurred in August 1965, when James Rouse was given permission to build Columbia.

James Rouse and Columbia

Columbia is one of America's largest planned cities. It isn't often that you hear about an entire new city being created. Yet that is how Columbia came to be. A man named James W. Rouse (1914–1996) bought

15,000 acres of farmland in 1963, and he decided to build a brand new city. His dream was that people from many different cultures and races would live and work in harmony there. In planning his city, he visited the Historical Society of Howard County, in Ellicott City, to learn the history of the county and to discuss his plans with some of the volunteers. He announced his plan in 1963, and was given approval in August 1965. In July 1967, the first people moved into their homes in this new city, in the Village of Wilde Lake. Eight more villages have since been built there. Rouse's plan called for each village in Columbia to have a shopping square, a swimming pool, and an elementary school. Today there are more than 78 miles of biking and hiking paths, 206 footbridges, and three man-made lakes where people can go sailing, boating, or fishing. Half of Howard County's businesses are currently located in Columbia.

The Columbia Association is a private, nonprofit, community service organization. It has a ten-member citizen-elected board of directors. These citizens represent the nine villages and the Town Center. They establish policies and handle financial matters. They also maintain all of Columbia's parks, bike paths, open areas, tot lots (playgrounds), lakes, health clubs, and other recreational facilities.

County Government

In the 1960s, the county decided to change the form of government it had used since its beginning. Citizens no longer elected commissioners. They adopted the charter form of government, which includes a county executive and a county council. This county government oversees all services, laws, and taxes, including those usually handled by towns or city councils. There are no town or city councils in Howard County, because there are no incorporated cities there.

The county executive is elected to a four-year term. He or she proposes and administers the budget. Among the county executive's many duties is carrying out county policy and working with state and other local governments.

The county council consists of five members from five different districts. These council members pass laws, handle the budgets, and help citizens solve problems.

Major Towns

Columbia is Howard County's largest city. It is where most of the businesses in the county are located. Columbia is interesting because it is divided into residential villages, each with its own special name.

Elk Ridge Landing was the first town built in what would become Howard County. It was a very busy port on the Patapsco River. Eventually, the name was changed to Elkridge. Elkridge is famous for an area known as Lawyer's Hill, where many old Victorian houses still stand. It also has a 120-year tradition of potluck suppers held by all the neighbors. This tradition started in the community hall, which was built after the Civil War to help people mend their differences about the war. In recent times the population has doubled, with many new homes.

Ellicott City began in 1772 when three Quaker brothers, Andrew, Joseph, and John Ellicott, moved to the area. They built several large mills for grinding wheat and making iron products. The town that grew up around the mills was called Ellicott's Mills. As the town became larger, the name was changed to Ellicott City. It is the county seat of Howard County. Many people visit Ellicott City every year to see its historic buildings and shop in the antique and other shops that line its streets.

Savage has long been famous for its textile mill, which was the only employer in the town for many years. The mill is now an antiques, crafts, and arts center.

The Lisbon/Glenelg area was once a busy market where farmers brought their produce to sell. Today, because agriculture is no longer the primary industry, farmers have opened riding stables, pick-your-own orchards, and country restaurants to earn their living.

North Laurel is located on the Patuxent River, which separates it from the city of Laurel in Prince George's County. In the 1800s, many farmers drove their horse-drawn wagons across the Patuxent River Bridge to the markets in Laurel.

Oella is a historic area on the Patapsco River centered around the textile mills that provided almost everyone a job. The original town was named after the first woman ever to spin cotton in America. The Union Manufacturing Company in Oella, for a short time, was the largest cotton mill in America.

West Friendship is the site of the Howard County Fair. The fairgrounds cover 25 acres.

Churches and Religion

The earliest church in what was to become Howard County was a Quaker meetinghouse at Elk Ridge Landing. It is believed to have been built around 1670. In 1800, that meetinghouse was abandoned and a new one was built. Other meetinghouses were also built in the area.

Episcopal and Methodist churches followed the Quaker meetinghouse. The first Episcopal congregation was that of Christ Episcopal Church, established in 1711. Its first services were held in a log cabin on what is now Oakland Mills Road.

Francis Asbury, a Methodist minister who would one day become a bishop, preached in Elkridge in 1772. It was the first church of his career. Catholic services were held in homes or private chapels before the American Revolution. Eventually, St. Louis Church in Clarksville was built, and then St. Paul's in Ellicott City in 1838.

In the early history of Howard County, Catholics were not allowed to celebrate mass. Therefore, the wealthier Catholic families built chapels on their own property. One of these was Doughoregan Manor Chapel, built by the Carroll family.

Black churches began to be established in the county about 1851. St. Luke's Church in Ellicott City and St. Stephen's in Elkridge were two of these early congregations. Other early churches include St. James United Methodist in West Friendship, Gaines African Methodist Episcopal in Elkridge, St. Michael's Roman Catholic in Poplar Springs, and St. Paul's Lutheran in Fulton.

Today in Howard County there are many different congregations. They include Catholic, Assembly of God, Lutheran, Presbyterian, Jewish, Islamic, Church of Christ, Mormon, Islam, Jehovah's Witnesses, Christian Science, Brethren, Seventh-Day Adventist, Baha'i,

Mennonite, Methodist A.M.E., United Methodist, Church of God, Baptist, Episcopal, Unitarian, Independent, interdenominational, interfaith centers, and many others. The idea for an interfaith center in Howard County came with the building of Columbia and its goal of friendship among people of different cultures.

<table>
<tr><td>FUN FACT</td><td>In 1914, the great baseball star Babe Ruth was married for the first time at St. Paul's Church in Ellicott City.</td><td></td></tr>
</table>

Education and Schools

During the earliest days of the county, there were no schools. Even in the early 1800s, families who could afford them had tutors for their children at home. Eventually in Elk Ridge an assembly room was built to be used as an entertainment center and a school. Another school followed, called Primary School Number One, which stood along the Washington Turnpike.

The Ellicotts started a school in Ellicott's Mills soon after settling there in the early 1700s, and were among the first to support education for black children in the area.

In 1816, the state general assembly passed an act to collect taxes that would be used for education. The hope was to provide education for poor children, who before this time were getting little or no education. After a state superintendent and school commissioners were appointed in 1825, counties were divided into school districts. In the region that would become Howard County, trustees were appointed to have schools built and maintained. Money was given to the schools, but it was often given unfairly. Some schools did not receive as much as others, and the quality of education was not equal. Eventually, state superintendent Reverend Libertus Van Bakklen established a new school system that was centralized in Annapolis and worked better.

More one-room schools were built. In 1868, plans were made for the first high school at Clarksville. It has since been torn down.

Patapsco Female Institute opened in 1837. It became a nationally known private school, and had students from all over America and even several foreign countries. Today it is on the National Register of Historic Places, because it was one of the first schools to educate young women. Many other private schools used to exist in the county, such as Rock Hill College, which burned down. The granite from that school was used to build Ellicott City High School on that same site. Weems School of Dundee was a school for girls. It was open for only ten years in the late 1800s. Estelle Kirkund's School was first located over her father's shoe store on Main Street.

In June 1870 it was decided that a portion of taxes paid by black families was to be used for education purposes. A few schools for black children were built, but they were not maintained as well as those for white children. The books used were old ones from the white schools. Black schools did not even get as much money for heating fuel as white schools. The teachers were paid only about half of the salary teachers at the white schools received. Until 1950, many black students had to go out of the county to go to high school. Cooksville High School was the only high school for black students in the county, and it was not an easy trip for everyone. In 1950, Harriet Tubman High School was built for black students. In 1954, the Supreme Court ruled that it was not legal to have separate schools for black children. Howard County, along with all other counties in Maryland, began desegregating its schools and sending children of all races to school together.

Since that time, Howard County's public school system has grown along with its population. The concept of neighborhood has been promoted by developers in Columbia who have donated money in every neighborhood to build an elementary school.

Howard County was one of the first counties in the state to build middle schools to replace junior high schools.   *FUN FACT*

Howard County Community College is a two-year college that offers an associate's degree. It has credit and noncredit courses. Other schools with branches in the county include Johns Hopkins University, Loyola College, and the University of Maryland.

Businesses, Industries, and Agriculture

The earliest businesses in the county were farms. Tobacco was grown and taken to Elk Ridge Landing, where it was shipped to Europe. Later on, mills started by the Ellicott brothers and others would bring success and fortune to their owners and workers. Other early businesses included iron furnaces and forges, which took advantage of the iron ore deposits in the county. Eventually, canning businesses, such as the Fleming and Sons Cannery, gave farmers another outlet for their vegetables. Dairy farming was popular. Farmers shipped the milk by train.

Today the farms in Howard County grow corn, wheat, barley, beans, soybeans, alfalfa, and hay. There are pick-your-own farms, where you can harvest your own apples, peaches, pears, raspberries, blackberries, and other small berries. The farms also grow vegetables such as tomatoes, cucumbers, beans, broccoli, and peppers. There are turf farms that grow sod (grass for lawns).

Landscaping is a big business in Howard County. Landscapers design outdoor areas and plant trees, bushes, and flowers to beautify the grounds of homes and businesses.

When the Ellicott brothers settled along the Patapsco River at what would become Ellicott City, they chose that spot for several reasons: location, a source of power, available markets for their goods and produce, and fertile soil for farms. Today, many farms and other businesses choose Howard County for the same reasons. An excellent system of roads, mass transit, and rail services are other reasons businesses open in the county. Many national and international businesses have located in Howard County and other areas in Central Maryland.

Employers include the Howard County public school system, which employs more than four thousand people. The Johns Hopkins Applied Physics Laboratory, Howard County government, Giant Food, Inc. Distribution Center, The Rouse Company, GSE Systems, Smelkinson Sysco, the Columbia Medical Plan, the Ryland Group, Inc., and W. R.

Grace and Company are other county-based businesses. There are many foreign-owned companies in the county. Among them is the Shimadzu Scientific Instrument Corporation, which has Japanese owners, and the Nucletron Corporation, which is Dutch-owned. People are also employed at hospitals, research centers, and various food distribution centers around the county. There are close to six thousand businesses in the county, most of which are in the Columbia area.

Because it is so close to interstate highways, mass transit by rail, airports, and the port of Baltimore, Howard County is well located for warehouses and distribution of goods. Many people who live in the county commute to work in Washington, D.C., Baltimore, or Frederick County.

Fascinating Folks (Past and Present)

Jonathan Ellicott (1756–1826) was responsible for planning and overseeing construction of the road that became the Baltimore-Frederick Turnpike, now Route 144.

George Ellicott (1760–1832) was an excellent mathematician and an amateur astronomer. He was concerned about the Indians in the area and wanted to make their lives better.

Charles Carroll usually ended his name with "of Carrollton." He was one of the four men from Maryland who signed the Declaration of Independence. He inherited Doughoregan Manor, a large estate that had been a land grant in the county. The Carroll family built a huge stone mansion on the property. In his later years, Carroll enjoyed spending his summers at his estate in Howard County, though his primary home was in Baltimore. The mansion is still owned by members of the Carroll family. Every Thanksgiving they hold fox hunts there.

The Ellicott brothers, who established Ellicott's Mills, were strong supporters of education. They opened a school for the children of the people who worked for them. The Ellicotts were among the first to believe that black children should be educated. Probably the most famous black child who attended the school they established was **Benjamin Banneker.** Banneker was born in 1731, in Baltimore County, and died in October 1806. He was a genius who educated himself in mathematics, astronomy, and science, with the help of books loaned to him by the

Ellicott brothers. He also learned to survey and was appointed to help plan the city of Washington, D.C. This made him the first black man appointed by the president to carry out a public service for his country.

It is believed that Banneker built the first striking clock made in Maryland. He did this after studying a watch given to him by a friend, Josef Levi. He carved most of the clock's parts from wood. This clock was so well built that it ran for many years. It even became an attraction for people to go to see.

Banneker also became famous for his almanac, called *Banneker's Almanac,* which was read throughout the United States and Europe. It contained weather predictions, essays, jokes, proverbs, and other interesting facts, just like Benjamin Franklin's almanac. In fact, some people say Benjamin Banneker looked very much like Benjamin Franklin. He was loved and respected for all his accomplishments by the people of Ellicott's Mills.

One of the young men guarding the Thomas Viaduct during the Civil War was sixteen-year-old **Louis LeClear.** While stationed there, he wrote to his mother about camp life. He told her that many things were being stolen. His musket had been stolen twice, although he got it back both times. His mess cup was stolen more than a dozen times and was always returned, until the last time. Once, a shoelace was stolen while he was sleeping. Louis became bored and wanted to join the twelve-man detail stationed at Ellicott's Mills. He eventually joined them in 1864 and wrote to his mother about what a great improvement there was in the food and housing.

There have been four men from Howard County who served as governors of Maryland. They are **George Howard** (1831–1833), **Thomas Watkins Ligon** (1854–1858), **John Lee Carroll** (1876–1880), and **Edwin Warfield** (1904–1908). Warfield was born in 1848 at "Oakdale" in Howard County. While he was governor he had the State

House in Annapolis restored to the condition it was in when George Washington resigned his commission as commander-in-chief of the Continental Army.

George Howard was born in the governor's mansion in Annapolis. This makes him the only son of a governor to be born in the mansion who eventually became governor himself. He moved to Howard County when he was married and received a piece of land there as a wedding gift. It was called Waverly.

FUN FACT

Bladen Yates owns the oldest business in Ellicott City. It was built by his grandfather, who started the grocery business in the late 1800s. The store was built around 1900. Yates and his wife also own the hardware store next door. These old stores are located across from the Fire House Museum.

Senator James Clark is a former state senator born in Howard County. While he was involved in politics, he was very interested in protecting the rights of farmers. He still owns a farm in the town of Clarksville, named after his family.

Buelah Buckner, nicknamed Meach, is the author of a book on black churches in Howard County.

Natural Resources

Howard County's most valuable resources are its two major rivers, the Patuxent and the Patapsco. In the past they have provided power to run the great mills that helped the county grow. Today they provide places where people can go to enjoy the beauty of the rivers and to picnic and fish. Bass are caught in the rivers, as are rainbow trout, brown trout, and other kinds of fish. Howard County also has beautiful lakes with fish such as sunfish and bluegills. Howard County's forests are another important resource, providing homes for wildlife and many plants.

Places of Interest

Historic Ellicott City is an eighteenth-century mill town on the Patapsco River. You can see historic buildings, such as the Thomas Isaac log cabin, built in the 1800s. George Ellicott's house, built in 1789, has been restored. Some of the buildings in Ellicott City were constructed with their foundations on either side of the river, which runs beneath the structures.

The **B & O Railroad Station Museum** is located on Maryland Avenue in Ellicott City. It was built in 1831 and is the oldest railroad station in America. The museum has Civil War artifacts and rifles. There is still graffiti written on the wall by soldiers on railroad guard duty during the Civil War. There are two waiting rooms, one for men, and one for women to care for their babies. In the freight house next to the station, there is a huge diorama (a scenic representation) of the first 13 miles of the B & O Railroad between Baltimore and Ellicott's Mills. Volunteers built the diorama over a three-year period. Visitors can go inside a caboose and see how the train conductors lived while "on the rails."

The **Firehouse Museum** is located on Church Road in Ellicott City. It was built at a cost of $500 in 1889, and served as a fire station until 1923. There is a two-wheeled hose cart that was pulled by hand up and down the hills of Ellicott City. Two bells that were used to signal a fire are also there. One was a gift to the firehouse museum from the B & O Railroad.

FUN FACT	"Big Bell" was loud enough to be heard throughout the city. Volunteer firemen would count the clangs of the bell, because different numbers of clangs signaled different locations.

The **Marlow House** on Hall Shop Road in Highland is a Civil War–era farmhouse built around 1840. The house has only one room on each of its two floors.

The **Patapsco Female Institute** on Church Road in Ellicott City first opened as a girls' school in 1837. Young women studied art, music, literature, science, and botany. It closed for a time during the Civil War, then reopened. It closed forever as a school in 1889. The building later became a hospital, a hotel, and a summer theater.

Merriweather Post Pavilion in Columbia is a large open-air theater known for its concert season and the many popular performers who appear there.

At the **Cider Mill and Petting Farm** in Elkridge, you can see how apple cider was made using a method called rack and cloth. Visitors can also enjoy petting and watching the farm animals.

Visitors to the **Thomas Viaduct** can easily imagine the old steam trains chugging along over the great stone bridge. It is on Levering Avenue near Elkridge.

Historic Savage Mill is a group of buildings constructed during the 1800s. The mill was founded in 1820 by Amos Williams and his three brothers. They named it Savage Mill after John Savage, who loaned them $20,000 to start the mill. Originally, the mill produced canvas for sails on clipper ships. During the Civil War, the material was used for tents and cannon covers. In later years, canvas was bought for backdrops (a cloth that hung across the back of a stage) for Hollywood silent movies. Today there are many craft shops, antique shops, and boutiques. On display is equipment that was used in the mills. The paymaster's office has been restored.

The **Howard County Historical Society Museum and Library** has a fascinating collection of historical artifacts, including photos, personal papers, weapons, and carpentry tools. It is housed in the former First Presbyterian Church building in Ellicott City on Court Avenue. The church was built in 1894 of huge granite blocks, with a spire that is more than 100 feet high. The library is in a separate building near the church. This building was a school for boys, built by the Ellicott brothers in the early 1800s. It is called the **Old Schoolhouse Building.**

The **Maryland Museum of African Art** in Columbia has exhibits and lectures about art from different countries in Africa and holds an "African Experience Tour." The museum was established in 1980 to help bring better understanding and appreciation of African-American art and culture.

The **Howard County Center of African-American Culture** in Columbia also exhibits African art and other cultural items representing the last two hundred years. It was founded in 1987 to collect, preserve, and interpret African-American culture in Howard County.

The **Ellicott City Colored School** is a one-room frame and clapboard schoolhouse built in the late 1880s for black children. It is about

48 by 30 feet and has a well, a pump, and two outhouses. To get there you have to cross a wooden bridge from Frederick Road. It has been restored as a monument to the many contributions of African-American people to Howard County.

Waverly is located in Woodstock. It was the property of John Eager Howard, the Revolutionary War hero, who was also governor of Maryland from 1788 to 1790. Howard County was named for him. His son George lived there when he married Prudence Ridgely of Hampton in 1811.

Visitors to Ellicott City can take a **Walking Tour of Ellicott City.** Stops on the tour include the Howard County Courthouse, built in 1841, and Emory Methodist Church, built in 1837. Mt. Ida, built in 1826, was the last house built by a member of the Ellicott family. Ellicott Cemetery is worth visiting, as is the Colonial Inn and Opera House. This may be where the actor John Wilkes Booth, who shot President Lincoln, first performed in this country.

Parks and Recreational Areas

The **Enchanted Forest** was a nursery-rhyme theme park that opened on Route 40 West in the mid-1950s. It featured huge Mother Goose figures. Just before the Enchanted Forest was due to open, Hurricane Connie hit Central Maryland. The park did open on schedule, but many of the shrubs, trees, and flowers that had been planted were destroyed and had to be replaced at a cost of several thousand dollars. The park closed in 1986. It reopened for a brief time in 1994, then closed again.

FUN FACT   The site of the Enchanted Forest was used as a setting in 1996 for an episode of the *Homicide* television series.

Patapsco Valley State Park is one of the two largest parks in the county that offers guided nature walks, canoe trips, and tube rides. You can also play ball on one of its ball fields.

Patuxent River State Park is most famous for its bird and nature hikes. You can also go tubing and canoeing along the river, play on the ball fields, or go on one of the guided nature walks.

Centennial Park has a two-mile jogging and walking path that goes around the man-made lake. There is a wildlife preserve, as well as picnic pavilions, boat rentals, and a refreshment stand.

Rockburn Branch Park has nature programs, hiking trails, picnic areas, and ball fields.

Savage Park features ball fields, picnic areas, hiking trails, and nature programs.

Kiwanis-Wallas Park has ball fields, a recreation center, and a senior center.

Schooley Mill Park is a 17-acre park featuring horseback riding, picnic areas, hiking trails, and different kinds of sports fields.

Howard County is known as "America's Heartland of Soccer" for several reasons. There are many soccer clubs in the county as well as strong recreational teams. A number of county players have gone on to the pros. Darryl Gee was a number two draft choice out of high school and played with the great Pele. Desmond Armstrong played in the 1996 Summer Olympics. In addition, there have been five national championships won by teams from Howard County. The 1997 under-18 team won the national championship and also were the defending champions from 1996.

FUN FACT

BIBLIOGRAPHY

Baltz, Shirley V. *The Quays of the City.* Annapolis, Md.: The Liberty Tree, Ltd., 1975.

Blount, R. Howard. *The Address Book of Children's Authors and Illustrators.* Minneapolis: T. S. Dennison and Company, Inc., 1992.

Board of Education of Anne Arundel County and Maryland State Department of Education. *Living in Anne Arundel County.* Maryland Picture Portfolio Series, vol. 2. Annapolis, Md.: 1962.

Boyd, T. H. S. *The History of Montgomery County from Its Earliest Settlement in 1650 to 1879.* Baltimore: Regional Publishing Company, 1972.

Bradford, James C., ed. *Anne Arundel County, Maryland: A Bicentennial History, 1649–1977.* Annapolis, Md.: Anne Arundel County and Annapolis Bicentennial Committee, 1977.

Burdett, Howard N. *Yesteryear in Annapolis.* Cambridge, Md.: Tidewater Publishers, 1974.

Coleman, Margaret Marshall. *Montgomery County: A Pictorial History.* Virginia Beach, Va.: The Donning Company Publishers, 1990.

Connell, Susan, ed. *Official Guide to Howard County.* Columbia, Md.: Patuxent Publishing Corporation, 1996–97.

Cramm, Joetta M. *A Pictorial History: Howard County.* Norfolk, Va.: The Donning Company Publishers, 1987.

Davis, David Brion. *Slavery in the Colonial Chesapeake.* Williamsburg, Va.: The Colonial Williamsburg Foundation, 1986.

Dozer, Donald Marquand. *Portrait of the Free State: A History of Maryland.* Cambridge, Md.: Tidewater Publishers, 1976.

Farquhar, Roger Brooke. *Old Homes and History of Montgomery County Maryland.* Silver Spring, Md.: Roger Brooke Farquhar Publisher, 1962.

Fradin, Dennis Brindell. *The Maryland Colony.* Chicago: Children's Press, 1990.

Kelly, Jacques. *Anne Arundel County: A Pictorial History.* Norfolk, Va.: The Donning Company Publishers, 1989.

Kent, Deborah. *America the Beautiful: Maryland.* Chicago: Children's Press, 1990.

Kibbler, Katherine, M. *The First 100 Years.* Annapolis, Md.: Anne Arundel County, Maryland, Board of Education, 1965.

Manakee, Harold R. *Maryland in the Civil War.* Baltimore: Maryland Historical Society, 1961.

Marek, John T. *Maryland, the Seventh State: A History.* Glen Arm, Md.: Creative Impressions, Ltd., 1995.

McDermott, Pamela, ed. *Green Acre School's Going Places with Children.* Rockville, Md.: Green Acres School, 1995.

McWilliams, Jane Wilson, and Carol C. Patton. *Bay Bridge on the Chesapeake.* Annapolis, Md.: Brighton Editions, 1986.

Mylander, Alison Ellicott. *The Ellicotts: Striving for a Holy Community.* Ellicott City, Md.: Historic Ellicott City, Inc., 1991.

National Aeronautics and Space Administration (NASA). *NASA, The First 25 Years, 1958–1983.* Washington, D.C.: NASA, 1984.

Rollo, Vera Foster, Ph.D. *Your Maryland: A History.* Lanham, Md.: Maryland Historical Press, 1993.

Schaun, George, and Virginia Schaun. *Biographical Sketches of Maryland.* Annapolis, Md.: Greenberry Publications, 1969.

Sween, Jane C. *Montgomery County: Two Centuries of Change.* Woodland Hills, Calif.: Windsor Publications, Inc., 1984.

Virta, Alan. *Prince George's County: A Pictorial History.* Virginia Beach, Va.: The Donning Company Publishers, 1991.

INDEX

Adams, John, 33
Adams, President John Quincy, 119
Advancement of Trade Act, 93, 94
Adventure World, 107–8
Agricultural Research Center, 97, 101
agriculture, 51, 74, 100, 115, 130
Aire, 94
Air Force One, 104
Alberton, 23
American Red Cross, 54, 56, 57, 116, 121
American Revolution. *See* Revolutionary
   War
American Telegraph, 28
Amtrak, 52
Anacostia River, 97
Anacostian Indians, 9, 10
Anderson, Brady, 103
Anderson, Horatio, 84
Andersonville National Cemetery (Georgia),
   117
Andrews Air Force Base, 62, 92, 104
Annapolis, 12, 20, 22, 24, 25, 28, 30, 31, 32,
   33, 36, 39, 75, 76, 77, 81, 84–90, 91, 97,
   128, 133
Annapolis and Elkridge Railroad, 27
Annapolis Junction, 27–8
Annapolis Short Line Rail Road, 28, 69
Anne Arundel County Free School, 82
Anne Arundel County Public Schools, 75
Anne Arundel Town, 20, 67, 75, 84
Annearrundell County Free School, 71, 73
Apollo 11, 85
archaeological sites, 8, 9
Armstrong, Desmond, 137
Armstrong, Neil, 82
Army Museum at Fort George G. Meade, 83
Arundell, Lady Anne, 67

Asbury, Francis, 127
Atlantic Coastal Plain, 3, 5, 16

B & O Railroad. *See* Baltimore and Ohio
   Railroad
B & O Railroad Station Museum, 134
Baldwin, Lt. Henry, 82
ballast, 14–5
Baltimore, 3, 25, 26, 27, 28, 36, 37, 43, 77,
   80, 96, 101, 124, 131, 134
Baltimore and Ohio Line, 28
Baltimore and Ohio Railroad, 26–7, 28, 50,
   119, 134
Baltimore and Potomac Railroad, 102, 107
Baltimore Colts, 78
Baltimore County, 123
Baltimore Orioles, 80, 103
Baltimore Ravens, 78
Baltimore/Washington International Airport,
   52, 69, 75, 80
Bancroft, George, 86, 87
Bancroft Hall, 87
Banneker, Benjamin, 17, 89, 131, 132
Barnesville, 113
Barney, Major William, 36
Barnum, P. T., 27
Barton, Clarissa Harlow (Clara), 54, 116–7,
   121
Battle of Bladensburg, 36
Battle of the Severn, 19
Bay Bridge. *See* William Preston Lane Me-
   morial Bridge
Bayne, Dr. John H., 102
Beall-Dawson House and Stonestreet
   Medical Museum, 120
Beanes, Dr. William, 36
Belair Mansion, 107

Belair Stable Museum, 101, 107
Belichick, Bill, 78
Belmont, 16
Belt, Truman, 97
Beltsville, 28, 46, 97
Bennett, Richard, 12
Bethel Methodist Episcopal Church South, 53
Bethesda, 5, 22, 112, 119
Bethlehem Steel, 101
Bigelow, Jacob, 41
Bird, Dr. Jacob W., 55
Blackistone, Mick, 79
Bladen, Governor Thomas, 77
Bladensburg, 28, 36, 55, 96, 98
Blair, Henry, 117
blue crab, 80
Board of Education of Prince George's
    County, 101
Bodkin Neck, 91
Bohl, Charles, 83
Bond, A. S., 44
Booth, John Wilkes, 48, 105, 136
Boston, Massachusetts, 29, 32
Boston Tea Party, 29
Boucher, Reverend John, 32
Bowe, Riddick, 103, 104
Bowie, 97, 107
Bowie, Captain Wat, 46
Bowie, Governor Oden, 97, 102
Bowie, Robert, 102
Boyds, 119, 120
Boyds Negro School House, 120
Brackenridge, Reverend John, 114
Bradford, Governor Augustus, 43, 44
Braxton, Toni, 78
brickmaking, 74
Briggs, Isaac, 117
Briggs, Nathan, 120
Britain. *See* England
Brooke, Dr. Richard, 102
Brooke, James, 15
Brooke Grove, 15
Brooke, Robert, 14
Brookeville, 37, 114
Brothers, Robert, 94
*Brown vs. the Board of Education of
    Topeka*, 99, 129
Brown, William, 82
Bryon, Dr. and Mrs. Paul, 120
Buchanan, Commander Franklin, 86
Buck House, 106

Buckland, William, 88
Buckner, Buelah, 133
businesses: Anne Arundel, 74; Howard,
    130–1; Montgomery, 115; Prince
    George's, 100–1
Butler, General Benjamin Franklin, 42–3, 47
Butler, Martha Purdy, 116
Butler, William H., 77
Byrd, Charlie, 78
Byrd, Harry Clifton, 100
Byrd Stadium, 100

C & O Canal. *See* Chesapeake and Ohio Canal
Cabin John, 113
Cabin John Creek, 42
Cabin John Park, 122
Cadwalladler, Sallie, 98, 99
Calvert, Cecil, 18, 19, 20, 67
Calvert, Charles, 19, 20, 67, 93
Calvert, Charles Benedict, 99, 100, 102
Calvert, George, 11, 102, 106
Calvert, Rosalie, 102, 106
Camp George G. Meade. *See* Fort Meade
Camp Parole, 44
Capital Center. *See* U.S. Air Arena
Carnes, Peter, 96
Carroll, Charles (of Carrollton), 25, 27,
    29–30, 31, 40, 75–6, 84, 91, 131
Carroll, Daniel, 34
Carroll, John, 97, 106, 113
Carroll, Governor John Lee, 132
Carson, Rachel, 118
Cary, Hettie, 43
Cary, Jennie, 43
Cash, Johnny, 83
Catholic Church, 12, 19, 93, 97, 106, 113
Centennial Park, 137
Challenger, 85
Chaney, Thomas D., 76
Chapel Hill School, 99
Charles Town, 93, 94, 97
Chase-Lloyd House, 76
Chase, Samuel, 31, 76, 84
Chesapeake and Ohio Canal, 26, 113, 119,
    120, 121, 122
Chesapeake Bay, 3, 4, 9, 31, 35, 80, 81, 82,
    91, 93
Chesapeake Bay Bridge. *See* William
    Preston Lane Memorial Bridge
Chesapeake log canoes, 23
Chestertown College, 98

Chevy Chase, 22, 112
Chittam's Addition to Bealle Town, 97
Christ Church, 112
Christ Episcopal Church, 127
Church of England, 12, 30, 94, 97
Churchill, John, Duke of Marlborough, 94
Church Road, 134
churches: Anne Arundel, 70–1, 75; Howard,
    127–8; Montgomery, 112–3; Prince
    George's, 97–8
Civil Service, 110
Civil War, 28, 42–7, 116–7; Anne Arundel
    42–4, 77, 82, 87; Howard 15, 46–7, 132,
    134, 135; Montgomery 46, 116–7; Prince
    George's 44–6, 95, 105
Claggett, Bishop Thomas John, 101
Claiborne, 81
Clara Barton National Historic Site, 121
Clark, Senator James, 133
Clarke, Noah Edward, 116
Clarksville, 23, 127, 129, 133
Clinton, 48, 108
climate, 3, 4, 5, 9
College Creek, 24
College Park, 99, 100
College Park Airport Museum, 105
Colonial Inn and Opera House, 136
colonial period, 21, 24
Columbia, 58, 123, 124–5, 126, 128, 129,
    131, 135
Confederate Army, 42
Congress. *See* U.S. Congress
Conrail, 52
Constitution. *See* U.S. Constitution
Constitutional Convention, 33
Constitutional Convention (Maryland), 44
Continental Army, 30, 33, 85, 101, 110, 133
Continental Congress, 31, 32, 76, 77, 84
Cooksville, 23, 129
Copley, Governor Lionel, 20, 70
county governments: Ann Arundel, 68–9;
    colonial county, 18; Howard, 125–6;
    Montgomery, 111; Prince George's,
    95–6
county seat: Anne Arundel, 67; Howard,
    124; Montgomery, 110 ; Prince
    George's, 93–5
courts, 60–2
Covington, Levin, 94
Cromwell, Oliver, 19
Crossland family, 84

crops, 4: colonial times, 12, 14, 15; Howard,
    130; Montgomery, 115; Prince George's,
    100
CSX, 52
Cumberland Road, 25
Cummings, Priscilla, 78

D'Alesandro, Mayor Thomas J., Jr., 80
Darnell, Henry, 106
Declaration of Independence, 31, 76, 84, 88,
    131
Della Brooke, 14
Democratic State Committee, 103
Dentzel Carousel, 121
desegregration, 114, 129
Dickerson, 121
Digges, Thomas Attwood, 32
Dinosaur Alley, 107
diseases, 31, 102, 113
District of Columbia. *See* Washington, D.C.
Dorsey, 112
Dorsey family, 16
Dorsey Furnace, 74
Doughoregan Manor, 25, 127, 131
Douglas, Justice William O., 120
Douglass, Frederick, 69, 82
Downs Memorial Park, 91
Drummer's Lot, 89–90
Durand, William, 12
Duvall, Gabriel, 106

earthfast homes, 13
Eastern Shore of Maryland, 19
Edben, William, 16
Eden, Governor, 86
education, 71–4, 98–9, 113–5, 128–30
elevation, 4, 5
Elk Ridge, 128
Elk Ridge Landing 15–6, 23, 126, 127, 130
Elkridge, 16, 102, 126, 127, 135
Ellicott, Andrew, 16, 17, 18, 126
Ellicott brothers, 16, 130, 131–2
Ellicott City, 23, 123, 124, 125, 126, 127,
    128, 130, 133–4, 135, 136
Ellicott, George, 131, 133–4
Ellicott, John, 16, 126
Ellicott, Jonathan, 131
Ellicott, Joseph, 16, 17, 18, 126
Ellicott, Judith, 18
Ellicott's Mills, 15, 23, 26, 27, 124, 126,
    128, 131, 132, 134

Elysville, 23
Emancipation Proclamation, 45
Emory Methodist Church, 136
England, 11, 19, 29, 30, 32, 33, 97, 98
English Parliament, 29
Estelle Kirkund's School, 129
exploration, 10–1

Fairmount Heights, 102
Fairview, 102
fall line, 5, 16
farmland, 4
Federalist, 85
fire departments, 64–5
Fire House Museum, 133, 134
First Presbyterian Church (Ellicott City),
    135
Fitzgerald, Francis Scott Key, 117
Fleming and Sons Cannery, 130
floods, Patapsco River, 17, 23
Fort George G. Meade, 53–4, 55, 83
Forest Glen, 22, 113
Fort Foote, 45
Fort Lincoln, 45
Fort Madison, 35
Fort McHenry, 37
Fort Meade. *See* Fort George G. Meade
Fort Nonsense, 82
Fort Severn, 35, 86
Ft. Washington, 32, 97, 103
Fort Washington National Park, 105
Fort Warburton, 105
Fox, George, 70
foundries, 33
Franklin, Benjamin, 33
Frederick, 124
Frederick County, 109, 131
Frederick County, Maryland Resolutions, 32
Freedman's Bureau, 72, 98
Friendship Airport. *See* Baltimore/Washing-
    ton International Airport
Friendship Church, 80
furnaces, iron, 16

Gaines Methodist Episcopal Church, 127
Gaithersburg, 5, 112
Garrett Park, 112
Gee, Darryl, 137
General Assembly. *See* Maryland General
    Assembly
General Committee, 32

Georgetown, 26, 33, 41, 121
geography, 3
German settlers, 109
Gillette, King Camp, 115
Glen Burnie, 70
Glen Echo, 117, 121
Glenelg, 126
Glenn Dale, 106
Glenn, Judge Elias, 70
Glenwood, 23
Goddard, Dr. Robert, 104–5
Goddard Space Flight Center, 51
gold mining, 50
Government House, 86
governments (county). *See* county govern-
    ments
Governor Ritchie Open Air Theater, 56
Governor's Mansion. *See* Government
    House
Grant, General Ulysses S., 48
Great Falls, 119, 121, 122
Great Seal of Maryland, 19
Great Seneca Park, 121
Greenbelt, 51, 108
Greenbury Point, 12
Greene, John W., Jr., 103
Groome, William, 93, 94
growing season, 4
Gullett, William W., 95
gunpowder, 33, 88

Hahn, Mary Downing, 103
Haley, Alex, 39, 88
Hammond-Harwood House, 88
Hanson, John, 52
Harness Creek, 90
Harriet Tubman High School, 129
Hartley, David, 33
Harundale, 70
Harwood, Sprigg, 44
Hawn, Goldie, 118
Henkle, Eli J,. 44
Henson, Josiah, 115–6
Hicks, Governor Thomas, 42–3
Highland, 134
Highland Beach, 69, 82–3
highways, 59–60
Hill, John Boynton Philip Clayton, 77
Hills Landing, 26
Hilton, 23
Historic Ellicott City, 133–4

Historic Savage Mill, 135
Historical Electronics Museum, 82
Historical Society of Howard County, 125
Historical Society of Prince George's
    County, 95, 102
Hockley, 16
Hogarth, 76
hogsheads, 12–3
Holly Hill, 76
homes, colonial, 13, 14
Hood, John 124
Hopkins, Johns, 71, 77
Howard County Center of African-American
    Culture, 135
Howard County Community College, 130
Howard County Courthouse, 136
Howard County Fair, 127
Howard County Historical Society Museum
    and Library, 135
House of Delegates, 84–5
Howard District of Anne Arundel County, 123
Howard, George, 136
Howard, Governor George, 124, 132, 133
Howard, John Eager, 123, 136
Hoyas basketball team, 107
Hubble Telescope, 104
Hughes, William, 124
hundreds (governmental division), 18, 95
Hungerford Resolves, 32
Hungerford's Tavern, 32, 110, 112
Hunt, Reverend James, 113
Huntington City, 97
Huntington Railroad Museum, 107
Hyatt, Christopher, 97
Hyattsville, 64–5, 97
Hyde, Thomas, 89

Ilchester, 23
Indians. See native peoples
indentured servants, 13, 38
industry, 51, 74, 100–1, 115, 130–1
International Red Cross, 117
Intolerable Acts, 29
iron, 74

J.A. Building/Olde Towne Tavern and
    Brewing Company, 112
Jackson, Andrew, 26
Jamestown, Virginia, 11
Jay, John, 33
Jefferson, Thomas, 106

Johns Hopkins Hospital, 77
Johns Hopkins University, 77, 130
Johnson, Walter Perry, 118
Jones, John Paul, 86
Jonestown, 23
Jug Bay Wetlands Sanctuary, 83

Kensington, 121
Kent Island, 81
Key, Francis Scott, 37
King James I, 11
King of France Tavern, 89
King William, 93
King Williams' School. See St. John's
    College
Kingsley Schoolhouse, 114
Kinte, Kunta, 39, 88, 90
Kiwanis-Wallas Park, 137
Klaus, Annette, 118
Kossman, Augusta, 55
Kunta Kinte Heritage Festival, 88

land grants, 15, 16, 131
Landover, 101
Lane, Governor William Preston, Jr., 80, 81
Largo, 99, 106
Latrobe, Benjamin Henry, 27, 116
Latrobe, John H. B., 27
Laurel, 28, 96, 98, 106, 126
Laurel Race Course, 82
Lavies, Bianca, 78
Lawyer's Hill, 126
LeClear, Louis, 132
Lee, Commander E. Brooke, 117
Lee, Ferdinand and Jane, 91
Leonard, Sugar Ray, 118
Leopard, 35
Levering Avenue, 135
Levi, Josef, 132
Lewis, Norm, 78
Liberty Tree, 88
life expectancy, 31, 48
lifestyles, 58–59
light rail, 52
Ligon, Governor Thomas Watkins, 132
Lincecomb, Thomas, 69
Lincoln, President Abraham, 42, 43, 44–5,
    48, 105, 136
Linthicum, 22, 69
Linthicum, Abner, 69
Linthicum Heights, 69

Lisbon, 23, 126
London Town, 25, 82
London Town Publik House, 82
Lords Baltimore, 93. *See also* Calverts
Lower Frederick County, 32, 109
loyalists, 33
Loyola College, 130

Madison, President James, 37
MacArthur, General Douglas, 24
Magothy River, 79
mail delivery, colonial period, 14, 15
Marlborough, 94
Marietta, 95, 102, 106
Marlow House, 134
Marshall Hall, 108
Marriottsville, 23
Maryland Agricultural College, 46, 99, 102
Maryland Assembly. *See* Maryland General Assembly
Maryland Clay Products Company, 107
Maryland Convention, 30
Maryland Gazette, 32
Maryland General Assembly, 12, 13, 18, 40, 66, 68, 81, 88, 95, 111, 113–4, 123, 124
Maryland Historical Press, 103
Maryland Inn, 89
Maryland Museum of African Art, 135
"Maryland, My Maryland," 43
Maryland–National Capital Park and Planning Commission, 95, 108, 120
Maryland Professional Baseball Players Association, 78
Maryland Resolutions, 110
Maryland State House, 33, 77, 84–5, 132–3
Maryland State Police, 62–3
Mason-Dixon Line, 46
Meadowside Nature Center, 122
Merkle Wildlife Sanctuary, 105
Merriweather Post Pavilion, 134
Methodists, 41
Miller, Oliver, 44
mills, 17, 23, 33
Mill Town, 94
Mitchellville, 107
Montgomery County Courthouse, 112
Montgomery County General Hospital, 55
Montgomery County Historical Society, 120
Montgomery, General Richard, 109–10
Montpelier Mansion, 93

Moore, Thomas, 116
Mookley Point, 108
Mormon Temple, 121
Morse, Samuel F. B., 28
Mount Airy Plantation, 108
Mount Calvert, 94
Mt. Helena Island, 44
Mt. Ida, 136
Mt. Misery, 44
Mt. Moriah A.M.E. Church, 89
Muirkirk Furnace, 101

NASA/Goddard Space Flight Center, 104
National Capital Trolley Museum, 121
National Colonial Farm, The, 106
National Register of Historic Places, 129
National Road, 25
National Security Agency, 54, 55, 56, 74, 83
National Wildlife Visitor's Center, 106
native peoples, 8–10, 11, 23, 88
natural resources, 5, 8, 79–80, 104, 118–9, 133
Naval Academy. *See* U.S. Naval Academy
Needwood Mansion, 120
Nichols, Reverend John, 53
Nicholson, Sir Francis, 20, 75
North Laurel, 126
Norwood, John, 64
Nottingham, 39, 94, 101
NSA. *See* National Security Agency

Oakdale, 132
occupations, colonial, 22, 24, 38
Odenton, 53, 78
Oella, 127
Ogle, Governor Samuel, 101
Old General's Highway, 81
Old Goshen Methodist Church, 120
Old Main Line, 47
Old Schoolhouse Building, 135
Old Senate Chamber, 33, 84, 85
Old Treasury, 85
Olmstead Bridges, 121
Owingsville, 23
Own's Ordinary, 112
oysters, 15, 74, 80

Paca, William, 31, 84, 88
Paris, France, 33
parishes (religious division), 18
parks, 90–1, 107–8, 121–2, 136–7

Partners in Flight, 119
Patapsco Female Institute, 55, 129, 134
Patapsco River, 25, 91, 126, 127, 133
Patapsco Valley State Park, 136
Patuxent Indians, 9
Patuxent River, 9, 16, 25, 26, 93, 96, 122, 126, 130, 133
Patuxent Wildlife Refuge, 51
Paul E. Garber Restoration Facility, 107
Peale, Charles, Wilson, 77
Peggy Stewart, 30, 76
Phelps, Babe, 78
Piedmont Plateau, 3, 4, 5, 16,
Pimlico Race Course, 102
Piscataway Creek, 97
Piscataway Indians, 9–10, 23
Piscataway Park, 108
plantations, 13, 31, 33, 38–9, 49
plants, 7
Plummer, Adam, 103
Plummer, Nellie Arnold, 49, 103
Poole's Tract, 114
Poolesville, 121
Poplar Springs, 23
population: Anne Arundel, 66; Howard, 123; Montgomery, 109; Prince George's, 92
Potomac, 118, 121
Potomac River, 9, 11, 25, 26, 33, 97, 104, 108, 119, 121, 122
Preakness, 102
Presbyterian Church, 113
Primary School Number One, 128
Prince George of Denmark, 93
Prince George's County Historical Society, 106
Prince George's Day, 93
Prince George's Parish, 112
Prince George's Seminary, 99
Princess Anne of England, 20, 93
Protestants, 20, 93
Providence, 12, 22, 67
Puritans, 12, 18–9, 22, 67

Quakers. *See* Society of Friends
Quaker Meeting House in Sandy Spring, 113
Queen Anne, 22
Queen Anne's Parish, 97
Queen Elizabeth, 100
Queen Mary, 93
Queen's Game, 100

Quiet Waters Park, 90

railroads, 16, 26–8
rainfall, 4, 5
Raleigh, Sir Walter, 11
Randall, James Ryder, 43
Reconstruction, 47
recreational areas: Anne Arundel, 90–1; Howard, 136–7; Montgomery,121–2 ; Prince George's, 107–8
Red Cross (house), 117
Red Cross. *See* American Red Cross
Relay, 26, 27
religious freedom, 12
Religious Toleration Act of 1649, 12, 18, 19
Revolutionary War, 29–33, 35, 52, 77, 85, 86, 89: Anne Arundel, 29–31, 76, 82, 83; Howard, 31, 127; Montgomery, 32–3 110; Prince George's, 31–2, 101
Rhode River, 25, 79
Ridgely, Prudence, 136
Riley Plantation, 115
Rising Sun Inn, 81
Ritchie, Governor Albert C., 52
Riversdale Estate, 28, 49, 95, 99, 102, 103, 106
roads, 23, 24–5
Robertson, William George, 120
Rockburn Branch Park, 137
Rock Creek, 41, 110
Rock Creek Chapel, 112
rocks, 4
Rock Hill College, 129
Rockville, 41, 46, 110, 112, 114, 115, 117, 119, 122
Rogers, James Harris, 54
Rogers, John, 31
roller coaster, 108
Rollo, Vera F., 103
Roosevelt, President Franklin D., 104
Rosaryville State Park, 108
Rose Hill, 49
Rouse, James W., 124–5
royal colony, 29
Ruth, Babe, 128

Sacred Heart-Whitemarsh Church, 97
Sandy Point, 81, 90
Sandy Spring Farmers Society, 115
schools, 71
Schooley Mill park, 137

Scott's Plantation (Belvoir), 81
Sajak, Pat, 78
St. Barnabas Church, 32
St. James United Methodist Church, 127
St. John's College, 44, 77, 87, 88, 98
St. John's Episcopal Church, 113
St. Louis Church, 127
St. Luke's Church, 127
St. Mary's Catholic Church, 113, 120
St. Mary's City, 12, 20, 67, 75
St. Mary's County, 12
St. Michael's Roman Catholic Church, 127
St. Paul's Church (Howard County), 127,
    128
St. Paul's Church (Prince George's County),
    94
St. Paul's Lutheran Church, 127
St. Paul's Parish, 97, 101
St. Stephen's Church, 127
Strawbridge, Robert, 113
Savage, 23, 126
Savage, John, 135
Savage Mill, 135
Savage Park, 137
schools: Anne Arundel, 71–4; Howard,
    128–30; Montgomery, 113–5; Prince
    George's, 98–9
Seneca Creek State Park, 121–2
Senaca Indians, 9
Seneca Schoolhouse, 114, 121
Senate Chamber (new), 84
settlement, 11–8: Anne Arundel, 11–4;
    homes, 13–4; Howard, 15–8; Montgom-
    ery, 14; Prince George's, 14
Severn, 78
Severn River, 11, 12, 22, 24
Severna Park, 69, 75, 79
Seymour, Governor, 22
Sharpe, Horatio, 86
Shaw, John, 77
sheriff's departments, 63–4
Short Line. See Annapolis Shortline Rail
    Road
Shrine of Our Lady of Fatima, 113
Silver Spring, 5, 103, 118
Simmons, Joseph, 76
Simpson, Charles R., 124
size of county: Anne Arundel, 4; Howard, 5;
    Montgomery, 5; Prince George's, 5
skipjacks, 74
slavery, 38–42, 44, 45, 100

Smith, Captain John, 9, 11, 79
Smith, Aunt Lucy, 76
Smithsonian Institution, 107, 118
Snowden, Nicholas, 96
Snowden Patuxent Ironworks, 74, 100
Society of Friends, 15, 40, 41, 46
soil, 4, 5
Sons of Liberty, 88
sotweed, 14
South River, 25, 82, 90, 91
Spa Creek, 24
Spanish-American War, 77
Spanish explorers, 10
springhouses, 14
Spurrier's Tavern, 81
Stack, Richard, 79
stagecoach, 24
Stanton, Edwin, 73
"Star-Spangled Banner," 36
State Circle, 88
State House. See Maryland State House
State Police. See Maryland State Police
steam engines, 27, 28
steamships, 25–6
Stewart, Anthony, 30, 76
Stewart, Peggy, 30
Stoddert, Benjamin, 101
Stone, Thomas, 31, 84
Stonestreet Medical Museum, 120
Stowe, Harriet Beecher, 116
Stratton,Charles Sherwood, 27
Suitland, 107
Supreme Court, 129
Surratt House, 48, 93, 95, 105
Surratt, Mary, 48
Surrattsville, 48
Susquehanna River, 9
Susquehannock Indians, 9, 23, 88

Takoma Park, 111, 118
Taylor, James H., 102
taverns, 22, 24: Harp and Crown, 24; King
    of France, 24
telegraph, 27, 28
temperance societies, 99
Thirteenth Amendment (U.S. Constitution),
    44
Thomas Issac log cabin, 133
Thomas, Philip E., 27
Thomas Point Lighthouse, 82, 91
Thomas Point Park, 91

Thomas Point Shoals, 82
Thomas Viaduct, 27, 47, 132, 135
tobacco, 12–3, 15, 16, 22, 25, 40, 74, 90, 94, 95, 100, 130
Tobacco Prise House, 90
Toleration Act. *See* Religious Toleration Act of 1649
Tom Thumb, 27
towns, establishment, 15, 22–3, 28: Anne Arundel, 69–70; Howard, 126–7; Montgomery, 111–2; Prince George's, 28, 96–7
transportation, 23–5, 52–3, 59–60
transportation, colonial, 14, 23–8
Treaty of Ghent, 36
Treaty of Paris, 33, 85, 89
Truman, President Harry S, 80
Truxton Park, 91
Tubman, Theodore, 124
Tuesday Club, 33
turnpikes, 24
turntable, 26
Tusculum, 113
Twin Oaks, 82

Uncle Tom's Cabin, 116
Underground Railroad, 41–2, 102
Union Army, 44, 45, 46, 105
Union Institute, 99
Union Manufacturing Company, 127
United Daughters of the Confederacy, 50
University of Maryland, 92, 93, 99–100, 101, 102, 106, 130
Upper Marlboro, 26, 36, 39, 55, 94, 105, 106
U.S. Air Arena, 106
U.S. Congress, 33, 34, 87
U.S. Constitution, 33–4, 85
U. S. Naval Academy, 30, 35, 43, 75, 77, 86–7
U.S.S. *Maryland,* 85

Van Bakkelen, Reverend Libertus, 72, 128
Village of Wilde Lake, 125

War of 1812, 35–7: Anne Arundel, 35, 36; Montgomery, 37; Prince George's, 36, 96, 105
Warburton Manor, 32
Warfield, Dr. Charles Alexander, 75
Warfield, Governor Edwin, 132

Warren, Edward, 96
Washington, Baltimore, and Annapolis Electric Railroad Company, 52
Washington Capitals (hockey team), 106–7
Washington County, 109
Washington, D.C., 3, 17, 27, 28, 34, 36, 45, 82, 93, 96, 110, 131, 132
Washington, George, 30, 33, 85, 108, 133
Washington Temple, 121
Washington Wizards, 107
Watkins Regional Park, 108
Waverly, 133, 36
weapons, 31
weather, 3, 4
Weems, George, 26
Weems School of Dundee, 129
Weems Steamboat Line, 26
Western Union Telegraph, 28
West Friendship, 23, 127
West River, 25, 79
West, Stephen, 31
Wheaton, 112, 119, 121
Wheaton, General Frank, 112
Wheaton Regional Park, 122
White's Ferry, 121
wildlife, 6, 80
William and Mary College, 98
William and Mary of England, 93
William Paca House and Gardens, 88
William Preston Lane Memorial Bridge, 68, 80–1, 90
Williams, Amos, 135
Williams, Montel, 83
Williams, "Parson" Rezin, 102
Williams, William Prather, 110
Williamsburg (in Montgomery County), 110
Wilmot, John, 71
Winder, General William H., 37
Women's Preparedness and Survey Committee, 54–5
Woodstock, 23
Woodward, William, 107
woolly mammoth, 8
World War I, 53–5, 117
World War II, 55–7, 67–8, 85, 104, 117, 124
Wright, Wilbur and Orville, 105

Yates, Bladen, 133
Yocacomico Indians, 9

Zubly, John Joachim, 76